Gardens of Historic CHARLESTON

James R. Cothran

University of South Carolina Press

Dedicated to Lynn and Caroline

Published in Columbia, South Carolina, by the
University of South Carolina Press

Printed in Canada

Library of Congress Cataloging-in-Publication Data

Cothran, James R., 1940–
        Gardens of historic Charleston / James R. Cothran
            p. cm.
        Includes bibliographical references and index.
        ISBN 1–57003–004–9
        1. Gardens—South Carolina—Charleston. I. Title.
SB466.U65C534 1995
712' .09757'915—dc20   94–18769

Viewed as a whole,
that bit of drifted yesterday
caught between time and
the rivers, called Charleston,
is a city set in a garden.

———

E. T. H. Shaffer,
Carolina Gardens, 1937

Contents

Preface

A decorative wall fountain adds the alluring sound of water to a Legare Street garden.

My first introduction to the gardens of historic Charleston occurred at an early age, resulting from a family visit in the late 1940s to tour the Lowcountry's legendary plantation gardens and to experience first hand the city's incomparable springtime display of camellias and azaleas. Memories of that visit remain vivid within my mind and, no doubt, as an adult have been responsible for drawing me back each year to renew the joys and pleasures associated with that early childhood experience. From these annual spring pilgrimages that have occurred over the last twenty years, I have developed a great love of Charleston gardens, especially the city's small town gardens which have their own special character and appeal. Thus, out of a passion for Charleston gardens and a compelling desire to share their beauty and charm with others was conceived the idea for this book.

On assembling material for this publication, I have endeavored to provide the reader with a comprehensive, yet concise, look at Charleston gardens in the context of a broad spectrum of cultural, historical, and physical factors which, over time, helped shape their development and design. Included in this discussion is an overview of Charleston's rich botanical and horticultural heritage that recognizes the special contributions by such notables as Mark

Catesby, Dr. Alexander Garden, André Michaux, John Champneys, and Joel Poinsett—to mention but a few. Charleston's rich garden tradition is also highlighted in the recognition of the gardens of Middleton Place and Magnolia Plantation plus the early gardening efforts of Thomas and Elizabeth Lamboll, Martha Logan, Henry Laurens, John Watson, and other important historical figures who helped shape Charleston's garden heritage. Special emphasis is also devoted to the tremendous influence on Charleston gardens by landscape architect Loutrel Briggs, who arrived in Charleston in the late 1920s and not only helped restore and preserve the spirit of many of Charleston's old and historic gardens but also created many new gardens whose designs have played a major role in establishing the city's distinctive garden style. Also included is a list of traditional plants which add beauty and magic to Charleston gardens and endow them with a special character and visual appeal.

A major focus of this book is Charleston's small town gardens for which the city is so famous. These unique outdoor spaces are the collective results of various physical factors including climate, architecture, enclosure, and the city's overall plan. Selected examples of Charleston's small town gardens are provided to emphasize the tremendous diversity and design possibilities that can be achieved within areas of limited space. These delightful "outdoor rooms" serve as an excellent source of contemporary ideas on how to achieve one's own personal and private world in an area of limited space. They also provide a wonderful source of inspiration and imaginative ideas for millions of Americans living in condominiums, town houses, and cluster homes or for anyone planning to create or improve a garden in a confined or restricted space. Much is gained from the experience and lessons in ingenuity and design represented in Charleston town gardens for it is here that small space gardening has reached its highest state of refinement.

Mimosa
(*Albizia julibrissin*)

Acknowledgments

Heyward Washington House Garden

Appreciation is extended to the following individuals who played an important role in making *Gardens of Historic Charleston* possible. These include Mrs. Emily Whaley, Mr. and Mrs. Owen Geer, Jr., Mr. and Mrs. Lloyd Wilcox, Mr. and Mrs. Andrew Drury, Mr. and Mrs. Joseph McGee, Mrs. Betsy Walker, Mrs. Robert Whitelaw, Mr. and Mrs. Theodore Guerard, Mr. and Mrs. John Avalon, Mr. and Mrs. Richard Coen, Mr. and Mrs. James Coker, Mr. and Mrs. Roger Hanahan, Dr. and Mrs. Bert Pruitt, and Mr. and Mrs. Harry Hugé, who graciously allowed their gardens to be featured in this publication.

I would also like to thank Kathryn Gaillard of the Charleston Museum, Patricia Bennett of the Charleston Library Society, and the dedicated staff of the South Carolina Historical Society, the Gibbes Museum of Art, and the Historic Charleston Foundation for their help and support. I am particularly indebted to Elise Pinckney of Charleston for her help with historic details and Clermont Lee of Savannah for her advice and consultation with plants. Additional thanks go to Marty Whaley Adams, Patti McGee, Mary Martha Blalock, and Jan McDougal for their contributions to my research efforts.

Special recognition goes to Charleston landscape architects Hugh and Mary Palmer Dargan, whose many fine garden designs and knowledge of Charleston's garden history greatly enriched this publication. Credit also goes to Alexander Wallace, whose artistic eye and photographic skills captured the beauty and charm of many of the gardens represented in this book. I am deeply indebted to Derek Fell for the generous use of selected photographs which dramatically portray the beauty and charm of Charleston's gardens.

Others to thank include: Terry Richardson for photography of museum art, Janet Tantum for permission to print illustrations from *Charleston Gardens*, and Mrs. William Coleman for her personal accounts of Loutrel Briggs. For their contributing support I wish to acknowledge the assistance of Robert Cuthbert IV, Bill McDougal, Karen Padgett Prewitt, Ron Huffman, and Robert Benson.

No account would be complete without recognition of several special individuals who gave freely of their time and talents in the production of text, illustration, and editing of *Gardens of Historic Charleston*. Foremost among these was Shirley Hallaron who deserves special recognition for her perseverance in typing manuscript changes. Diane Hachikian provided skilled assistance in the production of creative drawings of garden plans and illustrations and Mary Ann Eaddy did an outstanding job in the review of text and recommended editorial changes.

I am also grateful to Southern Living, the McMillan Press, Condé Nast Publications, Inc., the Library of Congress, the Smithsonian Institute's Archives of American Gardens, the Cherokee Garden Library, and the Hunt Institute of Botanical Documentation for their permission to use historical prints and photographs.

Finally, there are others too numerous to name who played an ongoing role in the research and production of this publication. Each is to be thanked for their support, assistance, and encouragement in making this book possible.

A view of the Heyward Washington House garden in late spring.

Overleaf: the Andrew Hasell House garden on a misty spring morning.

Gardens of Historic
CHARLESTON

Charleston's Horticultural Heritage

No place in America is endowed with a horticultural heritage as rich and diverse as Charleston and the Lowcountry of South Carolina. From the earliest of times explorers provided descriptive accounts of the abundant flora found in the area. As early as 1592 Laudonniere, a French explorer, offers one of the first glimpses of the Carolina coast: "We found the place as pleasant as possible, for it was covered with mighty oaks and infinite store of cedars and with Lentiskes [Myrtle] growing underneath them, smelling so sweetly, that the very fragrant odor made the land seem exceedingly pleasant. On every side were to be seen palm trees and other sorts of trees bearing blossoms of very rare shape and very good smell." Another account, this time by an English voyager almost one hundred years later, tells of "odoriferous and fragrant woods flourishing in perpetual and constant Vendure, vis. the lofty Pine, the sweet smelling Cedar and Cypress trees, the Wild Walnut or Hiquery Tree." Throughout Charleston's history a prominent group of naturalists, botanists, and plant collectors documented the region's rich natural heritage and played a significant role in expanding the knowledge of botany, horticulture, and gardening both in America and abroad.

One of the earliest naturalists to identify the native flora of the region was Mark Catesby (1679–1749), an Englishman who visited Charleston in 1722 and recorded finding "a country inferior to none in fertility, and abounding in variety of the blessings of nature." Catesby was kindly received by the Royal Governor and was introduced to the best of Charleston society. After surveying the local environs, he made a journey of forty miles "up the Country" to collect seeds and plants that later would be sent to England. The winter of 1723 to 1724 was spent in the neighborhood of Charleston, and by 1725, finding little new in the area, Catesby set off for the Bahama Islands. He returned to England in 1726 and in 1731 published a beautifully illustrated work entitled *The Natural History of Carolina, Florida, and the Bahama Islands;* a second volume was printed in 1743. These monumental works serve as landmarks of American fauna and flora and include first descriptions of many native American species of plants, herbs, fish, insects, and other forms of natural life. They also contain over two hundred illustrations from plates prepared by Catesby—a remarkable achievement for someone with little scientific knowledge and limited artistic training. Each plate was accompanied by text in both English and French. Representative shrubs and trees described by Catesby include the common catalpa (*Catalpa bignonioides*), often called the Indian bean-tree; the umbrella tree (*Magnolia tripetala*), one of the hardiest of the native magnolias; the fragrant sweetbay or swamp magnolia (*Magnolia virginiana*); the cherry laurel (*Prunus caroliniana*); the pink dogwood, a variety of *Cornus florida;* fringe tree (*Chionanthus virginicus*); and southern magnolia (*Magnolia grandiflora*), referred to by Catesby as the "laurel tree of Carolina."

Additional contributions to the knowledge of botany and the identification of plants were made by Dr. Alexander Garden (1728–1791). Born in Scotland and educated at the University of Edinburgh, Garden arrived in Charleston in 1752 where he practiced medicine for some thirty years. Edward McCrady in *History of South Carolina Under the Royal Government* describes Dr. Garden as "the most famous physician of Colonial times." Dr. Garden became an influential participant in Charleston's intellectual and cultural life and is credited with influencing the founding of the Charleston Museum, the earliest municipal museum in America. Dr. Garden was honored both in America and Europe for his outstanding contributions to the knowledge of American flora. In 1773 he was elected a fellow of The Royal Society of London for Improving Knowledge, an organization whose membership included men of eminent qualifications, both in Britain and the North American colonies.

Dr. Garden was a friend and correspondent with Linnaeus, the famous Swedish botanist, who established the modern system of plant classification, the Systema Naturae. Under this system plants are given two Latin names: the first one, the genus, and the second, the species. This simple but effective system of nomenclature helped to eliminate great confusion in the naming and identification of plants. It was Linnaeus who named the gardenia, or cape jasmine, in honor of Dr. Garden. Initially believed to be a native of the Cape of Good Hope, South Africa, the gardenia was later found to have its origin in China. It reached South Africa, no doubt, by way of an early sailing vessel that made its way from China to En-

The sweetbay, or swamp magnolia (*Magnolia virginiana*), from Mark Catesby's *The Natural History of Carolina, Florida, and the Bahama Islands.* The bird identified as the Blue Grosbeak was observed by Catesby "only in Carolina."

JASMINUM *rame uniflore, plene, petalis coriaceis.*

The gardenia (*Gardenia jasminoides*) was named by the Swedish botanist Linnaeus in honor of Dr. Alexander Garden, a Charleston physician and naturalist. Originally believed to be a native of the Cape of Good Hope, the gardenia was later found to have its origin in China.

ley County. His garden contained an elaborate system of winding walks and planting beds filled with indigenous plants. It was at Otranto that Dr. Garden cultivated many of the plants and seeds that he shipped abroad to various plant collectors with scientific interests in American flora. A list of seeds sent around 1760 by Dr. Garden to John Ellis, an Irish merchant and naturalist, included the silver-bell tree (*Halesia carolina*), loblolly bay (*Gordonia lasianthus*), sweet shrub (*Calycanthus floridus*), and the fringe tree (*Chionanthus virginicus*). Following the Revolutionary War, Dr. Garden, a Loyalist, was forced to leave Charleston because of his support for the king. He sailed for England in 1782 and died in London nine years later in 1791.

John Bartram (1699–1777), the noted American botanist and plant collector from Pennsylvania, exhibited a great interest in southern flora. Bartram developed the first botanical garden in America, along the Schuylkill River some three miles south of Philadelphia. He was well known for his frequent correspondence with other botanists in the colonies and abroad, including John Clayton of Virginia, Dr. Garden of Charleston, and Peter Collinson, an English woolen merchant who owned a celebrated eighteenth-century botanical garden in London. Through Collinson's influence, Bartram was appointed "His Majesty's Botanist for North America" under King George III. It was this fortuitous event that provided Bartram with an annual stipend of fifty pounds which enabled him to indulge his taste for travel and botanical exploration.

Bartram visited Charleston on several occasions in search of rare and unusual plants. His first trip took place in 1760 when he visited his friend Dr. Alexander Garden for eighteen days. During that visit Bartram roamed the woods and countryside and re-

gland. Gardenias have long been a favorite of Southern gardeners and were introduced into Charleston around 1762.

Dr. Garden maintained a nursery and garden at his plantation, Otranto, outside Charleston in Berke-

On a visit to Charleston in 1760, John Bartram collected a specimen of the great magnolia (*Magnolia grandiflora*) for his botanic garden in Philadelphia. Illustration from *The Natural History of Carolina, Florida, and the Bahama Islands* by Mark Catesby, courtesy of Colonial Williamsburg Foundation.

turned each day with plants which would later be shipped to Philadelphia. His collection included, among others, four umbrella trees (*Magnolia tripetala*) and a great magnolia (*Magnolia grandiflora*).

While in Charleston, Bartram spent several days visiting gardens and nurseries. He called upon Thomas Lamboll and his wife Elizabeth, who lived at the corner of King and Lamboll Streets. The Lambolls had developed a fine garden described as the first of its kind in Charleston and richly stored with flowers and vegetables. Thomas Lamboll is credited with introducing the chinaberry or pride of India (*Melia azedarach*) into Charleston. This fast-growing tree was often planted for shade along the city's foot paths and streets. Another garden visited by Bartram was that of Martha Logan. Described as a great florist and uncommonly fond of a garden, Logan was well known for her notable garden located on the Green, near Trott's Point. Although Bartram visited with Logan for only a brief period of time, it was sufficient to recognize that they shared a deep and abiding interest in plants that resulted in a mutual exchange of seeds, roots, and bulbs for many years to follow. In a letter to Collinson in 1761, Bartram writes, "I hope to have plants of it (the Cassine Holly) by the favour of an elderly widow lady (Mrs. Logan), who spares no pains nor costs to oblige me. Her garden is her delight. I was with her for about five minutes, in much company, yet we contracted such a mutual correspondence, that one silk bag hath passed and repassed full of seeds three times since last fall."

In 1765 John Bartram, along with his son William, visited Charleston again on their way to Georgia and Florida to conduct a plant expedition. His actual journey commenced on 1 July 1765 and continued until 10 April 1766. Bartram kept a detailed diary of his activities in which he wrote: "The inhabitants of both Carolina and Georgia generally build piazzas on one or more sides of their houses which is very commodious in these hot climates. They screen off the violent scorching sunshine and draw the breeze finely . . . and much conversation both sitting and walking is held in these." It was during this trip that Bartram discovered the Franklinia tree growing on the banks of the Altamaha River in Georgia. This unusual plant with pure white, saucer-shaped flowers and large yellow stamens was described by William Bartram as "a flowering tree of the first order for beauty and fragrance of blossoms." The Franklinia was last seen growing in the wild in 1803. Originally named *Gordonia pubescens*, its name was changed in 1785 to *Franklinia alatamaha* in honor of Benjamin Franklin.

Of all the botanists associated with Charleston's history, perhaps the most important was André Michaux (1746–1802), an intrepid French explorer and dedicated naturalist. Michaux conducted botanical expeditions in England, Auvergne, and Spain. From 1782 to 1785, under the auspices of the French government, he traveled widely in Persia from the Indian Ocean to the Caspian Sea. In 1785 Michaux returned to France with a magnificent collection of exotic Eastern plants and seeds. By way of a commission from Louis XVI, Michaux came to America in 1785 to collect flora from the New World that might have potential economic value to France. Plants collected in America were to be sent to the park at Rambouillet, located 20 miles south of Versailles, and to the Jardin des Plantes in Paris.

Michaux arrived in New York on 1 October 1785 with his fifteen-year-old son François and a gardener named Paul Saunier. After an unsuccessful attempt to set up a botanical garden in New Jersey, Michaux and his son moved to Charleston in 1787 where he established what would soon be called the French Garden, located about 10 miles outside Charleston at what was then known as the Goose Creek Parish. Michaux relocated to Charleston due to the mild climate which permitted botany and gardening to be carried on year around. From this garden Michaux cultivated many native plants collected from his travels that extended from southern Florida north to the Hudson Bay and westward to the Mississippi River. Michaux collected and described literally hundreds of native American plants. From Charleston, he shipped to France seeds and plants from the Carolinas that included loblolly bay (*Gordonia lasianthus*), yellow jessamine (*Gelsemium sempervirens*) which Michaux described as *Bignonia sempervirens*, Spanish bayonet (*Yucca gloriosa*), silver-bell tree (*Halesia carolina*), and the yellow flowered star anise (*Illicium parviflorum*). As a goodwill gesture to America, Michaux was allowed to bring from France a wide variety of exotic plants collected from all parts of the world. From both a historical and horticultural point of interest, Michaux's Charleston garden was especially important for it was from here that many old-world species were introduced into this country. Michaux is credited with bringing to America the fragrant tea olive (*Osmanthus fragrans*), the crape myrtle (*Lagerstroemia indica*), the Chinese tallow or candleberry tree (*Sapium sebiferum*), the mimosa or silk tree (*Albizia julibrissin*), the ginkgo or maidenhair tree (*Ginkgo biloba*), and according to legend, the camellia (*Camellia japonica*).

Following the French Revolution, funds to support Michaux's endeavors were sharply curtailed, eventually forcing him to leave Charleston in 1796 and return to France. In 1801 Michaux published a comprehensive study of American oaks. This was

The *Camellia japonica,* a traditional favorite in southern gardens, purportedly was introduced into Charleston before the end of the eighteenth century by the noted French botanist André Michaux (1746–1802).

François André Michaux (1770–1855)

As soon as I recovered from my illness, I left Charleston and went to reside in a small plantation about ten miles from the town, where my father had formed a botanical garden. It was there he collected and cultivated, with the greatest care, the plants that he found in the long and painful travels that his ardent love for science had urged him to make, almost every year in the different quarters of America. . . . I found in this garden a superb collection of trees and plants that had survived almost a total neglect for nearly the space of four years. I likewise found there a great number of trees belonging to the old continent, that my father had planted, some of which were in the most flourishing state.

André Michaux died in 1802 in Madagascar while conducting a plant expedition. His most important work, *Flora Boreali—Americana* (1803), the first comprehensive flora of North American plants, was completed by his son and published a year later. This outstanding work contains many illustrations by the famous botanical artist Pierre-Joseph Redouté.

Important contributions were made to the scientific knowledge of plants of the Charleston region by Thomas Walter (1740–1788), a native of England, who as a young man settled outside of Charleston along the Santee River. It was here that Walter developed one of America's first botanical gardens which contained over a thousand species of plants collected from a 25-mile radius. Walter was assisted by his friend John Fraser, a Scottish plant collector who first visited Charleston in 1784. Following Walter's death, Fraser returned to England with an unpublished manuscript which Walter had prepared on the flora of Carolina. This comprehensive work, published in London in 1788 under the title, *Flora Caroliniana*, represents the most complete work of American botany of the eighteenth century. Walter's

the same year that his son François, under the direction of the French minister of interior, returned to Charleston to ship all nursery stock remaining in the French Garden back to France. Upon arriving in Charleston, François became ill with yellow fever and was delayed for over a month. In his *Travels*, published in 1805, François wrote:

herbarium was purchased by the British Museum and, in appreciation of his outstanding scientific achievements, *Smilax walteri,* a beautiful red-berried vine found in the forest of the southern coastal plain was named in his honor.

Additional contributions to regional botany were made in 1798 by John Drayton, later to become governor of South Carolina, and in 1806 by Dr. John Shecut, noted Charleston physician and botanist. But it was not until 1821 and 1824 that a thorough work on local flora, entitled *Sketch of the Botany of South Carolina and Georgia,* was completed by Stephen Elliott—a Charleston resident, founding member of the Medical College of South Carolina and its first professor of botany and natural history.

Another important figure that played a significant role in Charleston's horticultural heritage was Eliza Lucas (1722–1793). Eliza was the daughter of George Lucas—a sugar planter and officer in the British Army who arrived in Charleston from the West Indies island of Antigua in 1738. George Lucas, who had inherited three South Carolina plantations from his father, decided to move his family to the smallest of these located on the Wapoo Creek, a few miles southeast of Charleston. Lucas hoped that the milder climate of South Carolina would help his ailing wife and that his family would be safe from the threat of Spanish invasion that existed in the West Indies. Lucas no sooner had settled in Charleston when in 1739 war broke out with Spain, and he was recalled to Antigua. He left his oldest daughter, Eliza, who was then only seventeen, in charge of the three plantations.

A bright and industrious young woman educated in England, Eliza Lucas exhibited a great interest in horticulture and gardening. In a letter to a friend she wrote, "I have a little library well furnished in which I spend part of my time. My music and the garden, which I am very fond of, take up the rest of my time that is not employed in business." Eliza Lucas also devoted a great deal of her efforts to developing indigo as a valuable export crop for South Carolina. The leaves of the indigo plant (*Indigofera suffruticosa*), a native of the West Indies, produce a dark blue dye that was in great demand in the English textile industry. The British had traditionally imported indigo from the French West Indies but through Eliza Lucas' efforts it became a valuable cash crop for South Carolina. Until the American Revolution the British government encouraged its production by placing a bounty of six pence on each pound purchased.

Eliza Lucas also experimented with cotton, Guiney corn, ginger, and alfalfa. She laid out a grove of live oak trees for timber production and planted a cedar grove, fig orchard, and flower garden. She also exchanged seeds and plants with her many acquaintances abroad and assisted Dr. Alexander Garden in the collection of specimens for identification and study. In 1744 she married Charles Pinckney, a successful lawyer and planter who shared her horticultural interest. Eliza Lucas Pinckney lived a long full life always experimenting with new crops and trees and even attempted to revive the silk culture with considerable success. Her two sons, Charles Cotesworth and Thomas Pinckney, became distinguished officers in the Revolutionary War. Charles later became a delegate to the Constitutional Convention and Thomas became governor of South Carolina. Both inherited their mother's interest in horticulture and love of plants. *Pinckneya pubens,* an unusual shrub or small tree only found in the southeastern United States, was named by André Michaux in honor of Charles Cotesworth Pinckney, a friend and associate, as a gesture of gratitude and respect.

An additional contribution to Charleston's hor-

Pinckneya pubens

First discovered by John and William Bartram on the banks of Georgia's Altamaha River in 1765, the *Pinckneya* was later described and named by André Michaux for his friend and associate Charles Cotesworth Pinckney (1746–1825) of South Carolina, a distinguished diplomat and general in the American Revolution. The most distinctive feature of the *Pinckneya,* both botanically and horticulturally, is the presence of brilliant, pink floral leaflets that occur in early summer, resembling those of the familiar Christmas poinsettia.

ticultural heritage was made by John Champneys (often misspelled Champney even by his contemporaries), a plantation owner and rice planter who maintained a large garden outside Charleston near Ravenel. David Ramsay, noted Charleston physician and historian, provides the following account of Champneys' garden in his *History of South Carolina,* around 1809:

> What was one of the most elaborate early gardens was in Saint Paul's district and was originally owned by William Williamson, but now belongs to John Champneys. It contains 26 acres, six of which are sheets of water and abound in excellent fish; ten acres in pleasure grounds are planted in every species of flowering trees, shrubs and flowers that this and the neighboring states can furnish: also with similar curious productions from Europe, Asia and Africa.

John Champneys exhibited a great interest in roses. Around 1811 he crossed *Rosa chinensis* (Old Blush) and *Rosa moschata,* a white musk rose, creating Champneys' Pink Cluster, the first rose to be hybridized in America. Champneys' Pink Cluster is a fragrant, semi-double rose with blooms that are carried in great clusters. While individual flowers are small, about 2 inches in diameter, in mass they create a spectacular display. Cuttings of the original plant were sent to William Prince of the famous Prince Nursery in Flushing, New York. Prince propagated Champneys' Pink Cluster for sale in the north and for distribution to nurserymen in England and France. Champneys also gave cuttings of his new rose to a friend and neighbor, Philippe Noissette, a French botanist and nurseryman who came to Charleston by way of Santo Domingo around 1793. Perceiving the commercial value of this new hybrid, Noissette soon grew plants for sale in the south. Philippe

Rosa Noisettiana.

Rosier de Philippe Noisette.

P.J. Redouté pinx.   Imprimerie de Rémond   Langlois sculp.

Pierre-Joseph Redouté (1759–1840), the most celebrated flower painter of the time, published his magnificent paintings of roses under the title of *Les roses.* Included in this monumental work is Champneys' Pink Cluster, identified by Redouté as *Rosa noisettiana* because of its close association with Philippe Noissette.

Joel Poinsett (1779–1851)

About 1828 Joel Poinsett, first U.S. ambassador to Mexico, introduced the poinsettia (*Euphorbia pulcherrima*) into Charleston. Since that time the poinsettia (facing page) has become a popular ornamental traditionally associated with the Christmas season.

Noissette also sent cuttings of the new rose to his brother Louis, who owned a nursery outside Paris. Louis began commercial production of the rose, and by 1820, Champneys' Pink Cluster was being widely grown in many parts of Europe. Louis crossed seedlings of Champneys' rose with other roses of the time to produce the class of roses known today as the Noisettes.

Joel Poinsett (1779–1851), a native Charlestonian and a descendant of a wealthy and well-known Huguenot family, was a leading gardener in the city around 1840. Poinsett was educated in Charleston and London and at Yale and was involved in the American diplomatic service. He was sent to South America as a confidential agent under President Madison and in 1824 was the first American minister to Mexico under President Jackson. As a result of his extensive travels and keen interest in plants, Poinsett supplied American nurseries with many unusual and exotic introductions.

Upon returning to Charleston, Poinsett maintained two gardens, a fine town garden on Rutledge Street and later a large garden on a plantation outside the city. In both Poinsett grew many interesting shrubs and trees collected from his travels. Around 1828 Poinsett distributed to several Charleston gardeners an unusual plant he found in Mexico. Characterized by colorful red leaves or bracts that looked like flowers, this striking plant, soon to be called poinsettia, drew the attention of a Colonel Carr, husband of John Bartram's granddaughter, Ann, while on a visit to Charleston. Colonel Carr arranged for the poinsettia to be exhibited in Philadelphia at the First Semi-Annual Exhibition of Fruits, Flowers, and Plants held in June 1829. It was here that Robert Buist (1805–1880), a prominent Philadelphia

nurseryman and florist, saw the poinsettia and began to propagate it as a greenhouse plant under the botanical name of *Poinsettia pulcherrima*. While the scientific name was later changed to *Euphorbia pulcherrima*, it continued to bear the common name poinsettia in honor of Joel Poinsett.

In 1850 Fredrika Bremer, a Swedish novelist who traveled widely throughout the United States, visited Joel Poinsett at his plantation home, Casa Bianca. This visit was arranged by Andrew Jackson Downing of New York, America's first landscape gardener and author of several books including *Treatise on the Theory and Practice of Landscape Gardening*. Published in 1841, when Downing was but twenty-six years old, this notable work played an important role in improving America's taste and awakening a sense of beauty regarding buildings, the cultivation of gardens, and the laying out of public grounds. No doubt Downing's theory and practice of landscape gardening had a profound influence on Poinsett for in Bremer's correspondence with her sister in Sweden she wrote, "round the house is a park or garden, rich in the most beautiful trees, shrubs and plants of the country, planted by Mr. Poinsett himself, according to Mr. Downing's advice."

John James Audubon (1785–1851), the famous American artist best known for his naturalistic paintings of birds, was closely associated with Charleston in the 1830s. It was during this time that Charleston served as a second home to Audubon and from which he painted many of the original watercolors included in his monumental work *The Birds of America*— one of the greatest achievements in American art. In addition to the 435 plates of species of American birds included in this admirable work are excellent representations of many native American trees, shrubs, vines, and flowers including the dahoon holly

(*Ilex cassine*), mountain laurel (*Kalmia latifolia*), tulip tree (*Liriodendron tulipifera*), live oak (*Quercus virginiana*), and trumpet creeper (*Campsis radicans*).

While in Charleston Audubon developed a close personal friendship with Reverend John Bachman, pastor of St. John's Lutheran Church and scientist in the field of ornithology. Audubon did much of his work from a ground floor studio at Bachman's home on Rutledge Street that overlooked a lush garden containing woodbine (*Lonicera sempervirens*), dogwood, and cherokee roses collected from the woods. John Bachman assisted Audubon with his writing and sketches and often accompanied him into the fields to secure specimens to paint. Bachman's sister-in-law, Maria Martin, was commissioned to paint flowers and plants as backgrounds in at least twenty of Audubon's paintings of birds. It was from this close association with John Bachman and Maria Martin that many of Audubon's prints reflect plants, natural habitats and local scenes associated with Charleston and the Carolina Lowcountry.

Charleston's horticultural knowledge was greatly enhanced by the founding of the Charleston Library Society in 1748. By 1770 the Society had in its possession an impressive collection of well-known botanical books and plant references. This extensive collection of early works in botany and gardening speaks well of the city's interest in horticulture and landscape gardening. Included in the collection were Catesby's *Natural History of Carolina, Florida, and the Bahama Islands*, Miller's *Gardener's Dictionary*, and sixteen volumes of *Linnaei*. By 1826 many additional books had been added: *Observations on Modern Gardening, Planting and Rural Ornament, A Sketch of the Botany of South Carolina and Geor-*

Bachman's Warbler from John James Audubon's *The Birds of America*

"My friend Bachman has the merit of having discovered this pretty little species of Warbler, and to him I have the pleasure of acknowledging my obligations for the pair which you will find represented in the plate, accompanied with a figure of the most beautiful of our southern flowers (*Franklinia alatamaha*) originally drawn by my friend's sister, Miss Martin."

Audubon, 1834
(*Ornithological Biography,* vol. 2)

A plate from Dezallier d'Argenville's *The Theory and Practice of Gardening,* 1712

This comprehensive work contains plans and designs used in the layout of fine gardens commonly referred to as "pleasure gardens."

gia, *The Carolina Florist, American Medical Botany,* and *The Theory and Practice of Gardening* (first published in Paris in 1709 and translated into English in 1712). This latter, handsomely illustrated work helped to establish the standards for developing fine gardens during the time (1734–1766) when many English planters of South Carolina were laying out their estates along the Ashley and Cooper Rivers. Included in this book were advice and recommendations on design elements—such as garden size, views, parterres, walks, groves, bowling greens, canals, and statuary—which could be employed to "distinguish a garden very much from what is common and contribute not a little to render it magnificent."

While Charleston gardeners initially obtained bulbs, roots, and seeds for their gardens from England and other European sources, this practice soon waned as a greater selection of imported and locally grown material was made available through Charleston suppliers. This is evidenced in the ever increasing number of advertisements in local newspapers which were used by local seed dealers and nurserymen to market their wares.

As early as 1732 Samuel Everleigh, one of Charleston's earliest seed dealers, offered for sale in the *South Carolina Gazette* (Charleston's first newspaper), "divers sorts of best Garden seeds." A second advertisement in the same publication appeared in 1735 again noting the availability of "Garden seeds fresh and good."

(*South Carolina Gazette,* 23–30 December 1732; *South Carolina Gazette,* 3 January 1735)

In 1745 Richard Lake offered for sale at his plantation on the Ashley River "Lemon Trees, with Lemons on them in Boxes, Lime Trees and Orange Trees in Boxes, and several curious Plants in Pots, also a variety of young Fruit Trees."

(*South Carolina Gazette*, 15 September 1745)

In 1753 Martha Logan, one of Charleston's most distinguished gardeners and daughter of Robert Daniels, deputy governor of South Carolina, advertised for sale "seeds, flower roots, and fruit stones." In 1768, some fifteen years following her initial advertisement, Logan was still in business, offering "a Fresh Assortment of very good garden seeds and flower roots . . . with flowering shrubs and box for edging beds."

(*South Carolina Gazette*, November 1753;
South Carolina Gazette, 14 March 1768)

John Watson, an English gardener who arrived in Charleston around 1755, became one of the most successful nursery owners and seed merchants in Charleston. In 1765 Watson advertised for sale "a great variety of Tulips, hiacynths, lilies, anemonies, ranocluses, double jonquils." In 1786 he offered for sale a "great variety of Seeds and Plants of flowering Trees, Shrubs, Evergreens . . . and the natural growth of South Carolina."

(*South Carolina Gazette*, 10 November 1765)

Robert Squibb, a respected Charleston gardener and owner of one of the city's earliest nurseries, advertised local seed for sale. In the advertisement, Squibb, who was convinced of the greater viability of locally grown seed, advised "against depending on foreign seed, in particular such as onions, carrots, parsnip, parsley, celery, lettuce, endive, and spinage." Squibb's advice was no doubt greatly respected for in 1787 he authored *The Gardener's Calender*, the second work on gardening published in America. This informative document provided southern gardeners with invaluable information on what to plant each month for best possible results.

(*City Gazette and the Daily Advisor*, 19 August 1795)

Charleston could boast a botanic garden as early as 1805. Laid out on land provided by Mary Savage, the garden soon would be known as the Charleston Botanic Society and Garden. The garden was financed by dues from its members as well as funds contributed by the Medical Society of Charleston—no doubt to encourage the growing of plants with potential value to the medical field. It is conceivable that knowledge gained from this endeavor assisted Dr. Francis Porcher, a Charleston physician, who in 1863 was commissioned by the Confederate surgeon general to gather information on the medicinal qualities of plants for use by Army surgeons during the Civil War. Dr. Porcher's book, *Resources of the Southern Fields and Forests*, provides a comprehensive list of plants describing their medicinal and practical value.

Dr. Porcher's efforts primarily were directed at recommending substitutes for imported medicines from plant sources that could easily be obtained in every part of the country. Included in his exhaustive list of plants with medicinal qualities were sassafras (*Sassafras albidum*) from whose leaves and roots a tea could be made for use in the treatment of measles, pneumonia, bronchitis, and colds; dogwood (*Cornus florida*) whose bark was employed with great advantage as a substitute for quinine, particularly in cases of low forms of fever and dysentery; and American holly (*Ilex opaca*) whose bark served both as a tonic and a treatment for coughs and colds.

The Charleston Botanic Garden flourished for a number of years under the direction of a botanist-gardener and several assistants. The *Charleston Directory of 1809* lists Philippe Noissette as the director. The garden contained many indigenous and imported plants and was laid out according to the Linnean system. Plants were obtained from American naturalists as well as from plant collectors and distributors from abroad. It can be assumed that this garden played an important role in furthering the knowledge and use of many unusual and exotic plants in Charleston during the nineteenth century.

Charleston also exhibited a great interest in the development of parks and open space. Charles Fraser (1782–1860), a Charleston lawyer and artist best known for his miniature portraits and paintings of local Charleston scenes, provides in his *Reminiscences of Charleston* a description of some of the city's open spaces or greens as they appeared around 1800:

> There was a word then, and for some years afterward, known in our topography, now no longer used, towit: "a green" to denote large vacant places along the margin of the town. Some of these were "College Green," "Bouquet's Green," and "Harlestone's Green." I must not omit to mention "Gadsden's Green" which was a vacant space surrounding the residence of General Gadsden. . . . There was another lot or green on the south side of Tradd Street . . . I remember it as Squibb's garden. . . . City square was opened in 1818—it is now a beautiful walk of shade trees.

By 1840 many of these old greens or open spaces where children had played and troops had drilled were filled in to make room for new houses and public buildings.

White Point Garden, or the Battery, as it is frequently called, is one of Charleston's most historic open spaces. This modern day park is located along South Battery to King Street at the southern end of the city. The site dates back to the city's earliest records when the names White Point and Oyster Point were given to the area because of the abundance of oyster shells and white sand found on the point of the peninsula. Oyster shells were present in such quantity that in 1690 a law was enacted requiring that they be used to cover the streets and thoroughfares of the city. The name "battery" commemorates the fortifications of earthworks and batteries that were placed on the site during the Revolutionary War, the War of 1812, and the Civil War.

A comprehensive plan was prepared for White Point Garden in 1837 by New York architect, Charles F. Reichardt. It was hailed by Charleston's newspaper, *The News and Courier*, as a visionary scheme that would produce "a public promenade or garden covering an area of three acres of ground, sufficiently accessible to the sea breeze, commanding the same prospect adverted to, and unsurpassed in beauty, and in all the sources of recreation, by any similar spot in the United States." In 1906 landscape architect John Charles Olmsted (1852–1920), the stepson of

A View near Charleston, 1801. Where St. Paul's Church now stands, Ratcliffe lands by Charles Fraser (watercolor on paper)

Charles Fraser (1782–1860), a distinguished Charleston artist, captured in his sketchbook views of churches, plantation houses, and landscape scenes in and around the city.

Frederick Law Olmsted who designed Central Park and the gardens and grounds of Biltmore Estate, visited Charleston to confer with the city on various design changes to White Point Garden. Olmsted advised against the use of shrubs and flowers in the park and urged reliance on the simple beauty of grass and trees. This policy has prevailed, and the park is today a pleasant expanse of green lawn and a beautiful canopy of live oak trees (*Quercus virginiana*).

The Olmsted firm was retained by the city to assist with the design of a park system which included Chicora, Cannon, and Hampton Parks. The latter was the former site of the South Carolina Interstate and West Indian Exposition of 1901 which included lakes, gardens, and a variety of exhibitions directed at bringing industry and commerce to the city. Plans for Hampton Park prepared by the Olmsted firm included a tree-lined driveway around the entire park, rustic arbors, beautiful playgrounds for children, several small lakes, a creek for boats, and various other innovations.

Tree planting along Charleston's streets was a

common practice as observed by John Charles Olmsted in 1910, "There are many trees in the old streets but the sidewalks are so narrow and the houses so generally built directly on the street line that the trees are generally planted in the roadway where, of course, they are much damaged. . . . The most popular tree in the streets seems to be the southern elm [*Ulmus alata*] which with its small leaf certainly had the advantage of not casting so deep a shade over windows as most other trees." Other historic trees which were often planted along Charleston's streets included the hackberry (*Celtis laevigata*), palmetto (*Sabal palmetto*), live oak (*Quercus virginiana*), and during colonial times the chinaberry or Pride of India (*Melia azedarach*) described by André Michaux in 1790 as affording the inhabitants excellent shade from the sun. It was not until 1915 that the city's park commission initiated the narrowing of streets and the planting of trees inside the curb to protect them against horses and vehicles—a practice which had been previously adopted by many northern cities with great satisfaction.

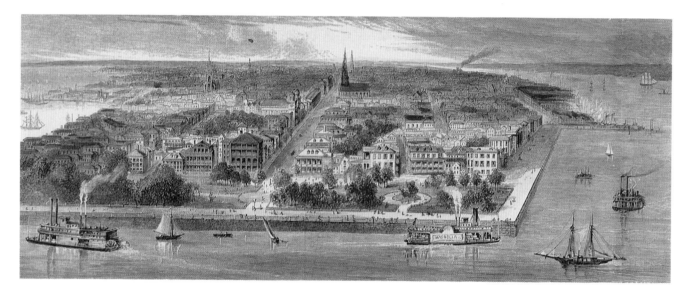

Charleston From the Bay from *Picturesque America;* courtesy of the Charleston Museum, Charleston, South Carolina

"Charleston has been accused of not having a public park; but the promenade known as the Battery is an enclosure which, if small, has some advantages that very few parks can supply. . . . It commands a view of the extensive bay, and is fanned by winds that come laden with the salt odors of the ocean. It is surrounded by fine mansions, and at early morning, at twilight, or on moonlit nights, is thronged with people seeking rest and relaxation."

Picturesque America (1874)

White Point Garden is one of Charleston's most historic open
spaces. A view down the central promenade showing
monuments, live oak trees (*Quercus virginiana*), and
Charleston Battery benches which were added around 1880.

Charleston's Garden Tradition

Charleston has a rich garden heritage dating from colonial times. In 1682, only two years after the city was established at its present location on the peninsula between the Ashley and Cooper Rivers, the English chronicler Thomas Ashe, in a document entitled *Carolina, or a Description of the Present State of That Country,* observed that early English settlers were already securing plants from the old world for both practical and ornamental use: "their Gardens begin to be supplied with such European Plants and Herbs as are necessary for the Kitchen, viz: Potatoes, Lettuce, Colewarts, Parsnip, Turnip, Carrot and Radish; Their gardens also began to be beautified and adorned with such Herbs and Flowers which to the Smell or Eye are pleasing and agreeable, viz: the Rose, Tulip, Carnation and Lilly, Etc."

Charleston soon became the center of gardening in the southern colonies, and some of the country's finest houses and gardens were built outside the city along the Ashley and Cooper Rivers. These large estates, known as plantations, were developed by cultured English planters who had acquired their fortunes in agriculture or trade in the Carolinas and the West Indies. These wealthy landowners soon set out to build fine houses and gardens in the English tradition. Prominent among these early plantations were Mulberry, Mepkin, Crowfield, Middleburg, and Glebe along the Cooper River and Cedar Grove, Newington, Middleton Place, Drayton Hall, and Magnolia on the Ashley. The building of large houses and elaborate gardens was made possible by a favorable climate, an abundant source of slave labor, and economic prosperity that resulted from the cultivation of rice, indigo, and cotton.

Charleston's early gardens were greatly influenced by European landscape design. England's gardens at the time Charleston was settled were very French and formal in character in the style of André Le Nôtre with central and cross axes, decorative parterres, straight walks, statuary, elaborate fountains, and canals. With the arrival of William III of Holland to the English throne in 1689, England's gardens assumed many characteristics inherent to the Dutch style of landscape design. While similar in many respects to the gardens of Renaissance France, Dutch gardens, as a rule, were smaller and more intimate in scale. They were often enclosed by walls or hedges, had simpler parterres, more topiary, and relied to a greater extent on the use of flowers, bulbs, and ornamental plants. Fine gardens, like the stately country houses of England during this period, were an important part of life and culture and represented symbols of wealth, power, and social prestige. It was

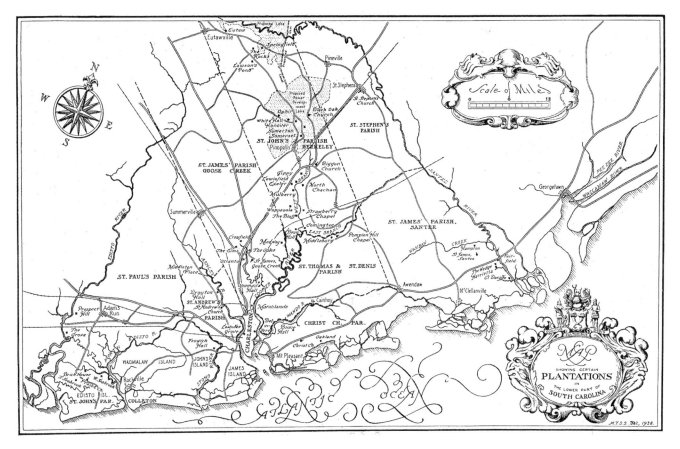

A map showing the location of plantations of the Carolina Lowcountry and their geographic relation to Charleston. Charleston historian Samuel Gaillard Stoney observed that "the Ashley River two centuries ago was the Thames, the Loire of South Carolina. All the great men of that time then aspired to build Palladian villas along its course and surround them with gardens in the manner of Le Nôtre."

this idealized model of grand houses and gardens that was to play an important role in the development of Charleston's gardens throughout the colonial period. Influenced as they were by European garden styles and designs, the unique surroundings and climate of the Carolina Lowcountry gave Charleston's gardens a distinctive character and flavor all their own.

Of the more than seventy or so plantations that once existed along the Ashley and Cooper Rivers, one of the finest was Crowfield Plantation. The original tract of land on which Crowfield was built was originally owned by John Berringer, a native of Barbados. The property was eventually purchased by Arthur Middleton, who gave it as a gift to his elder son, Williams, in 1729. In 1730 Williams Middleton built a brick manor house along with 20 acres of formal gardens and ornamental grounds. The plan of Crowfield was reminiscent of an early English country estate with fine house and garden and was laid out in an elegant fashion so as to convey the social and economic position enjoyed by its owner. Its reputation soon became famous throughout America and abroad.

In 1743 Eliza Lucas visited Crowfield plantation and described its celebrated garden in a letter to her friend, Miss Bartlett, in London:

> The first we arrived at was Crowfield, Mr. Wm. Middleton's seat, where we spent a most agreeable week. The house stands a mile from but in sight of the road, and makes a very handsome appearance; as you draw nearer new beauties discover themselves; first the beautiful vine mantling the wall, laden with delicious clusters, next a large pond in the midst of a spacious green presents itself as you enter the gate. The house is well furnished, the rooms well contrived and elegantly furnished. From the back door is a wide walk a thousand feet long, each side of which nearest the house is a grass plat ornamented in a serpentine manner with flowers; next to that on the right hand is what immediately struck my rural taste, a thicket of young, tall live oaks. Opposite on the left hand is a large square boleing green, sunk a little below the level of the rest of the garden, with a walk quite round bordered by a double row of fine large flowering Laurel and Catalpas— which afford both shade and beauty. My letter will be of unreasonable length if I don't pass over the mounts, wilderness, etc., and come to the boundary of this charming spot, where is a large fish pond with a mount rising out of the middle the top of which is level with the dwelling house, and upon it is a Roman temple. On each side are other large fish ponds, properly disposed which form a fine prospect of water from the house—beyond this are the smiling fields dressed in vivid green.

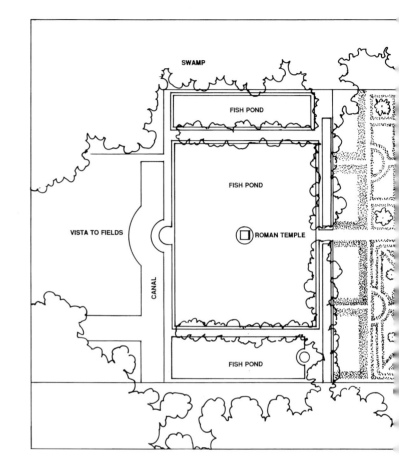

In 1753 Williams Middleton advertised in the *South Carolina Gazette* that he planned to return to England and desired to sell Crowfield which he described as "containing about 1,800 acres of land (the most of it good for either rice, corn or indigo) whereon is a large brick dwelling house with many convenient out-houses and a neat regular garden." By 1845 Crowfield had ceased to function as a working plantation, and in 1886 Crowfield Hall was destroyed by a devastating earthquake. Today there is

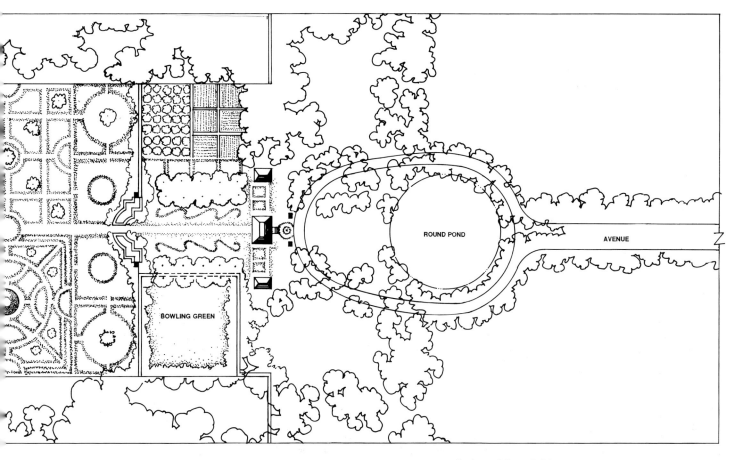

ROUND POND

AVENUE

BOWLING GREEN

A plan of Crowfield depicting the garden layout with conjectural design.

little that remains of the garden or grounds.

Of the many fine eighteenth-century gardens that once existed outside of Charleston, Henry Middleton's great garden on the Ashley River is the only one that survived. Often described as the premier garden of colonial America, Middleton Place was built about 1741 by Henry Middleton, who later became president of the First Continental Congress. Not to be outdone by his brother Williams, who developed the extensive gardens at Crowfield Planta-

25

An aerial view of Middleton Place showing its central axis connecting the entrance drive, terraces, butterfly lakes, and the Ashley River beyond (photographed at Middleton Place, Charleston, South Carolina).

tion, Henry sent to England for an experienced landscape gardener to lay out the gardens at Middleton Place in the grand style that was in fashion in England during the seventeenth and early eighteenth centuries.

Conceived in a bold and expansive manner unparalleled in colonial America, the gardens covered over 40 acres and required the labor of one hundred slaves who toiled for over ten years to create the grassy terraces, butterfly lakes, groves, formal walks, allées, and canal. The design of Middleton Place gardens is a remarkable example of genius and geometry, perfectly suited and adapted to the contours and the lay of the land. The sitting of the manor house and gardens along a central axis, extending from the arrival gate through the main dwelling and gardens to the Ashley River and the low land beyond, is in itself an outstanding work of art. The garden plan reveals that the Ashley River served as the primary approach to the house which was reached by way of a balanced plan of walks and terraces following a direct line to the entrance of the manor house.

To the north of the house lies a series of gardens collectively contained by rice fields, reflecting pools, and forest edges. Divided by parallel and perpendicular paths and allées, these individual gardens fit with geometric precision into the framework of a right triangle. Included in this collection of gardens is a sunken octagonal garden, once used as a bowling green; a rose garden designed in the shape of a wheel; the remains of a mount which at one time offered a superb view of the gardens and the marshlands beyond; and several secret gardens which originally were quite formal in design with box-bordered beds, walks,

Middleton Place garden plan. Surveyed and drawn by A. T. S. Stoney in 1938.

A view of the surviving wing of the original manor house with a magnificent planting of *Azalea indica* added to the gardens by Williams Middleton in 1846.

and paths. Nearby lays the majestic Middleton oak which for centuries has stood like a sentinel towering over the gardens and the events which shaped Middleton's illustrious past.

While strictly adhering to the layout of the original plan, descendants of Henry Middleton have over the years added a variety of additional plants. André Michaux, the noted French botanist, often visited Middleton Plantation bringing with him many rare and unusual plants. Tradition has it that he introduced at Middleton four of the first camellias (*Camellia japonica*) successfully grown outside in an American garden—several of which still survive. Additional plantings of camellias were later added in

the 1830s. When Williams Middleton, an attaché of the American Legation in Russia and a signer of the Ordinance of Secession, inherited the estate in 1846, he greatly enhanced the gardens by adding magnificent plantings of southern Indian azaleas (*Azalea indica*).

While Middleton Place has been subjected to the destructive forces of wars, earthquakes, hurricanes, and the adversities of time, its magnificent gardens have miraculously survived. This has resulted in part due to the enduring strength and continuity of their design as reflected in the magnificent display of grand terraces, graceful reflecting pools, ornamental lakes, and classical patterned gardens that exist in total and complete harmony with the land.

The ancient estate of Magnolia-on-the-Ashley represents another outstanding, but contrasting, example of garden development that occurred several miles south of Middleton Place. Named for the long avenue of magnolias (*Magnolia grandiflora*) that once stretched to the Ashley River, Magnolia Plantation has been in continuous ownership of the Drayton family, their ancestors and descendants, since 1670. The original mansion was burned by British soldiers during the Revolutionary War, and a second house met a similar fate at the hands of Union troops at the close of the Civil War. The small pre-revolutionary structure which presently exists at Magnolia Plantation was relocated from nearby Summerville shortly after 1865.

Little remains of the original formal garden except a small section, known as Flowerdale, dating from the 1680s. The gardens as they are known to-

A small picturesque cottage stands sentinel over Magnolia Plantation on the site of an earlier house that was destroyed during the Civil War.

Unlike the formality of Middleton Place, the gardens at Magnolia were developed along natural and gentle lines that conformed to the English naturalistic style of design.

lia are now gigantic in size and are the true glory of the gardens in spring. In addition to azaleas, Rev. John Drayton imported and planted many camellias (*Camellia japonica*) which by 1860 totaled over 120 varieties. The gardens are at their best in early spring when the riotous blooms of azaleas, camellias, wisteria (*Wisteria sinensis*), yellow jessamine, and the Cherokee rose (*Rosa laevigata*) are reflected in the dark still waters of the Lowcountry forest creating a haunting and unforgettable landscape scene that has been appropriately described as "a sunlit cathedral" and "a picture too beautiful to paint."

Fine gardens were by no means limited to the grand estates outside of Charleston but were equally prominent within the city as well. One of the first town gardens to be recorded was that of Mrs. Thomas Lamboll about 1750. Mrs. Lamboll planted a large and handsome flower and kitchen garden upon the European plan on the west side of King Street about the present location of Lamboll Street. Another early garden was planted by Martha Logan on Meeting Street. Logan is credited with writing the first American gardening book, *The Gardener's Kalendar,* which influenced the practice of gardening in and around Charleston until the early nineteenth century. In 1755 Henry Laurens, a leading citizen in Charleston, built a town house on East Bay Street in a section called Ansonborough. It was here that Laurens developed a 4-acre garden that was enclosed by a brick wall 200 yards long and 150 yards wide. Contained within the garden were both useful and ornamental plants from the Carolinas as well as imported plants which his mercantile con-

day were redesigned by Rev. John Grimke Drayton, Episcopal clergyman and gardener extraordinaire, along softer and more natural lines. Under the influence of the informal school of English landscape design (1715–1830), the gardens at Magnolia Plantation were reshaped to include winding paths, sinuous lakes, and informal plantings of exotic trees and shrubs. The first southern Indian azaleas (*Azalea indica*) were planted there around 1843. It is speculated that these original plants were obtained from Philadelphia and included varieties with distinct English names such as Prince of Wales, Fielder's White, Glory of Sunninghill, and Pride of Dorking. Many of the original specimens planted at Magno-

Magnolia Gardens are an enchanted wilderness of brilliant azaleas, camellias, wisteria, and live oaks amid a verdant carpet of green.

nection had enabled him to obtain from remote corners of the world. Laurens introduced into South Carolina olives, capers, limes, ginger, guinea grass, alpine strawberries, red raspberries, blue grapes, and various fruits from southern France. In 1765 John Bartram visited Laurens and noted that he was making great improvements in gardening. Laurens himself wrote in 1775 that his garden looked as charming as any garden could look. The garden was superintended with maternal care by Laurens' wife, Elinor, who was assisted by John Watson, a trained English gardener, who later developed his own garden on Trott's Point. Watson is credited with establishing the first nursery in the city where he sold flowers, seed, shrubs, and native plants as well as garden tools. He also did gardening in all its branches—in town or country, by the day or the year.

Plans of many of Charleston's early town gardens are contained in the record books of property transfers of the eighteenth and early nineteenth centuries. These documents, known as the *John McCrady Plat Books,* provide descriptions of many garden plans as well as building layouts and property boundaries. In almost every case these early gardens were enclosed by brick walls in the English tradition and were laid out in simple geometric patterns of square and rectangular beds, occasionally with a small circle as a central feature in the design. These early town gardens were generally located at the rear or side of the property and often included an orchard, vegetable, and flower garden in formal designs. In Charleston, as was the case in England, ownership of a flower garden and orchard was a sign of gentility. Items typically grown in Charleston's early gardens included apple, quince, pear, plum, nectarine, apricot, peach, olives, grapes, figs, pomegranates, oranges, lemons, and limes. Many early gardens were built on lots that were quite large, often encompassing an entire square or half square, thus providing ample space to separate the garden from various out-

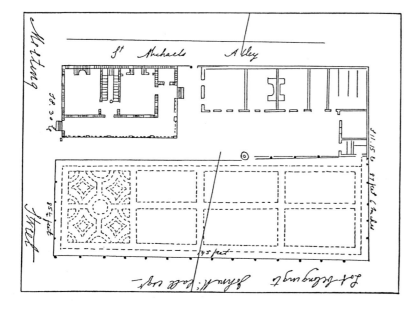

Judge Elihu Hall Bay's Garden

The plan of the garden, courtesy of the Charleston Museum, Charleston, South Carolina, was obtained from a survey made in 1789, when the property was in the ownership of Judge Elihu Hall Bay. Located at the southeast corner of Meeting Street and St. Michael's Place, the walled garden was approximately 86 feet wide and 145 feet long. The design of the flower garden reflected a geometric pattern composed of a series of half circles and diamonds positioned around a circular motif. The six rectangular beds comprising the remainder of the garden served as fruit and kitchen gardens.

buildings (kitchen, servant quarters, stables, carriage house, privy) which were separate features of the house and garden plan. A typical garden of this period was owned by Alexander Gordon, clerk of the council in 1749, on a lot that contained two full acres of land. The garden was "genteelly laid out in walks and allées, with flower-knots and laid round with bricks, having also several kinds of fruit trees now bearing, and many orange trees." In time as the city grew, these large building lots and gardens were reduced in size by the filling in of creeks and low-lying areas and the construction of new streets, houses, and public buildings.

Charleston's passion for gardening during the colonial and post-Revolutionary period is evidenced by numerous advertisements describing the services and talents of professional gardeners available to assist in the laying out of gardens and ornamental grounds:

"Mr. Peter Chassereau, newly came from London . . . sets out ground for Gardens or Parks, in a grand and rural manner."

(*South Carolina Gazette*, 4 January 1734)

"This is to give Notice to Such Gentlemen and others as have a taste in pleasure and kitchen gardens, that they may depend on having them laid out, leveled and drained, in the most complete manner, and the politest taste, by the subscriber; who perfectly understands the contriving of all kinds of new works, and erecting water works, such as fountains, cascades, grottos."

(John Barnes, Garden-Architect, *South Carolina Gazette*, 25 February–3 March 1764)

"The Subscriber takes this method to acquaint the Publisher, that he will undertake to MAKE, or put in COMPLETE ORDER, the GARDEN of any Gentlemen or LADY in or within two or three miles of Charleston, at an Easy Expense, . . . and can be well recommended by the Gentlemen he came out of England with."

(William Bennett, *South Carolina* and *American General Gazette*, 13–20 May 1771)

"WANTS A PLACE, A FRENCH GARDENER, from Paris, having been in this Country three or four years, during which time he was greatly improved under the skillful Mr. Michaux, the French botanist . . . at length he knows every line of his profession, and to conclude he is very well recommended."

(*The Charleston City Gazette*, 7 November 1794)

"The Subscriber, well acquainted with the European method of gardening, being a native of England, and likewise well acquainted with it in this state . . . proposes superintending ladies and gentlemen's gardens in or near the city whether intended for pleasure or profit— he also plans and lays out gardens in the European taste on moderate terms."

(J. Bryant, *The Charleston City Gazette*, 6 June 1795)

In addition to an increasing number of itinerant gardeners who arrived from Europe to assist in the design of Charleston's plantation and town gardens, contributions were also made to the fields of horticulture and gardening by the French Huguenots who had immigrated to Charleston by 1700. Many of these early French settlers were artisans by trade and often became gardeners for the large plantations that developed along the Ashley and Cooper Rivers.

Those that settled in the city were particularly well known for their fine small gardens and for their influence on the design of many of Charleston's town gardens during the eighteenth and early nineteenth century.

One of the most notable and frequently mentioned of Charleston's colonial town gardens was that of the Miles Brewton House located on the west side of lower King Street. Built around 1769 by Miles

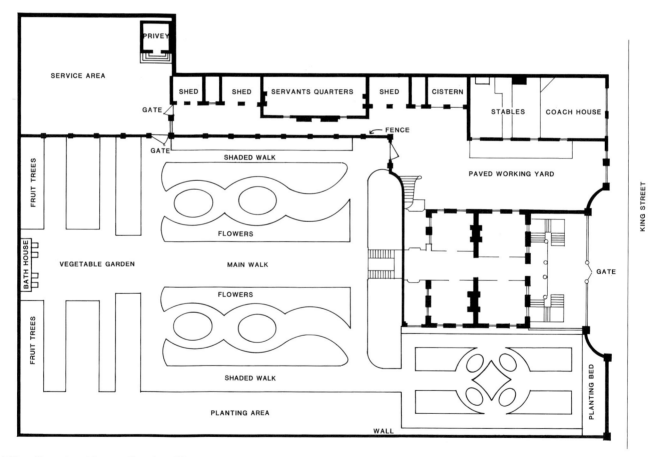

Miles Brewton House Garden Plan

Brewton, a wealthy Charleston merchant, the house has been described as a supreme example of a double house in the city and one of the finest town houses in America. The garden's earliest plan indicates that it was designed along a main axis that extended from the house to a central focal point—a decorative pavilion complete with marble columns, located at the western extremity of the site. The garden originally extended all the way to Legare Street.

The main garden, surrounded by brick walls 8 to 10 feet high, was based on a unified design; an upper garden devoted to flowers and ornamental plants with a lower garden relegated to vegetables and fruit trees. An additional area to the south of the house served as a pleasure garden, while the area to the north was given over entirely to utilitarian needs, including servant quarters, kitchen, stables, carriage house, and cistern. A later version of the original plan indicates that the garden underwent an elaborate redesign around 1857 when the rear portion of the property was sold. The new garden contained a more intricate arrangement of brick-bordered beds in paisley designs. Plants that were grown in this garden included pomegranates, figs, oleanders, mimosa, vitex, sweet shrub, gardenias, altheas, acacia (*Acacia farnesiana*), star jasmine and a variety of old roses, including Duke of Luxemborg, Safrano, and Devoniensis.

A re-created town garden of the colonial era can be found on Church Street at the Heyward-Washington House. This fine old double house was built in 1770 and was owned by Thomas Heyward, Jr., a signer of the Declaration of Independence. In May 1791 President George Washington was housed in the Heyward House during his visit to Charleston as part of his triumphant tour of the South. While no record of

Miles Brewton House Garden

"Down the center goes a wide pathway. . . . The flower beds extend on either side, brick-edged and bordered with sweet violets and other small and fragrant plants. Close to the house the oleanders and acacias bloom and crowd, and vines are all about clambering over porches and walls and trees. So secluded is it that the wild songbirds come here to nest, careless of the city close around."
Hildegarde Hawthorne, *The Lure of the Garden*

the original garden plan survived, the existing garden was carefully researched and laid out in the 1930s in a fashion that exemplifies a late eighteenth-century Charleston garden. The garden incorporates a series of circles in a symmetrical design. Paths are of sandshell, and the five patterned beds are bordered with old Charleston brick and edged with Harland boxwood to maintain the design. Beds are planted with heirloom flowers, bulbs, and ornamental shrubs of the period including such favorites as violas, tulips, scilla, candytuft, stock, calendulas, and stokesia.

Charleston gardens suffered immeasurably during the Revolutionary War years (1775–1783). Records reveal that British soldiers stationed in the vicinity of Middleton Place amused themselves with breaking the heads from the marble statues that adorned the grounds. The exquisite gardens at the Grove, located on Charleston Neck, were also destroyed and it is reported that their owner, John Gibbes, died in grief when he viewed the waste. The extensive town gardens of Henry Laurens and John Watson were also ruined. Tradition has it that during the siege of the city in 1780 Henry's son, Colonel John Laurens, and his light infantry repaired breaches in their fortification with choice exotic and fine shrubbery from his father's East Bay garden.

Following the destructive effects of the Revolutionary War, Charleston soon regained its position as a major port. With increased planting of rice and long-staple Sea Island cotton, prosperity soon returned. Shortly after the American Revolution, houses built in Charleston began to depart from the established types and included piazzas or open galleries that extended the entire length of the house on the south or west sides. In *Charleston, the Place and the People*, Harriott Rutledge Ravenel provides a description of the city around 1790:

> The Houses many of them wood and airy, and the fashion of piazzas was becoming general. People were adopting the peculiar style of house stretched long to catch the breeze with gable end to the street and long piazzas. It was not as handsome but cooler and better suited to the climate than the square colonial mansion. This manner of house presupposes a garden, for the door upon the street is in truth only a sort of gate, and the true front door opens from the piazza, and gives upon the garden opposite. . . . In the town, behind their high walls grew oleanders and pome-

The Heyward-Washington House garden is a re-creation of a late eighteenth-century Charleston garden. Its formal design and use of heirloom plants create an air of antiquity and old-world charm.

granates, figs and grapes, and orange trees both sweet and bitter, and bulbs brought from Holland, jonquils and hyacinths. The air was fragrant with the sweet olive, myrtle and gardenia. There were old-fashioned roses! the cinnamon, the York and Lancaster, the little white musk, and the sweet or Damascus. The glossy-leaved Cherokee clothed the walls with its great white disks, and was crowned by jasmine and honeysuckle.

During the early part of the nineteenth century many wealthy plantation owners built fine town houses in Charleston to escape the ravages of malaria that plagued the river swamps and lowlands from May through November. Many of these town houses were quite grand in scale and often included elaborate gardens in formal designs. Owning a house in Charleston not only offered freedom from the threat of malaria but also provided the opportunity to become a part of the social life of the city as well. Social interaction between planters and urban gentry, no doubt, fostered a fruitful exchange of information on horticulture and gardening to include books, plants, nursery sources, garden theory, and design. While England's gardens during this period had become informal as a result of the influence of the naturalistic style of design, Charleston's gardeners generally adhered to the formality that was popular during earlier times. Gardens, with few exceptions (notably Magnolia Plantation), continued to maintain geometric regularity in layout and design. As evidence of Charleston's continuing interest in gardens, the *City Directory of 1809* listed no less than sixteen professional gardeners available to as-

"A passion for flowers has of late astonishingly increased. Many families in the capital and many in the country, for some years past, have been uncommonly attentive to flower gardens. Those who cannot command convenient spots of ground have their piazzas, balconies and windows richly adorned with the beauties of nature far beyond anything that was known in the days of their infancy."

David Ramsey, Charleston historian and physician, ca. 1804 (*The History of South Carolina*)

The Jenkins Mikell House with its formal gardens was built in 1853 by Edisto Island cotton planter I. Jenkins Mikell. Designed in the elegant manner of an Italian villa, the Jenkins Mikell House represents one of the last great town houses built in Charleston before the end of the antebellum era.

sist with the layout and planting of gardens and grounds.

Descriptions of several town gardens in Charleston during the early nineteenth century are provided by Alice Lockwood in *Gardens of Colony and State*. This comprehensive work, prepared in two volumes by the Garden Club of America, documents the gardens and gardeners of the American Colonies and of the Republic before 1840. One of the most important Charleston gardens during the early 1800s as described in this work was that of Governor Thomas Bennett who brought over two English gardeners to whom he gave a house and a yearly salary of twelve hundred dollars. "The garden was the governor's pride. . . . The grounds were most extensive, including a vegetable garden in the rear, numerous fruit trees and a group of large Live Oaks. The garden was laid out in the Flemish style, square beds and broad, straight walks. Many foreign plants were brought from Europe; they were constantly being added to by things strange and beautiful. There were extensive greenhouses in which delicate plants were kept, and pineapples were raised." One of Governor Bennett's gardeners, Andrew Gray, developed a beautiful yellow Noisette rose (believed to be a seedling of Cloth of Gold) which he named Isabella Gray in honor of his wife.

Another important garden of this period was that of Mrs. William A. Hayne. Located on the corner of Ashley Avenue and Cannon Street, the garden was described as very formal with box-bordered flower beds in shapes of diamonds.

> At one end of the garden were three pieces of topiary. . . . At the other end and at each side were large lattice trellises covered with white and yellow climbing roses. Large *Camellia japonica* trees, white, red and variegated, single and double varieties, were planted in favorable spots. . . . A row of magnolias with their handsome white and purple blossoms stood at the rear of the garden, and every available space was filled with roses, day lilies, clove pinks, and other small sweet-scented plants. Many of the box beds were filled with a delightful variety of spring bulbs. The garden was separated from the street by an open wooden fence, and the paths were of pounded white oyster shells.

The Nathaniel Russell House on Meeting Street also contained an elegant nineteenth-century garden. The house was built by Nathaniel Russell, a prominent shipping merchant from Rhode Island, at a cost of $80,000 and completed in 1809 when Russell was

In a Charleston Garden by Anna Whelan Betts

seventy-one years of age. Russell maintained a large garden in a geometric arrangement with patterned beds of flowers, ornamental shrubs, and large orange and grapefruit trees. In 1819 William Faux, an English traveller and author of *Memorable Days in America*, tells of a visit with the venerable Russell only a year before his death in 1820. Russell was found "living in a splendid mansion surrounded by

Nathaniel Russell House Garden

For a number of years the Nathaniel Russell House served as the Convent of the Sisters of Mercy. Hildegarde Hawthorne described the garden during that time as "lovely with pomegranates, with spikenard (*Vitex agnus-castus*), the pale shadowy tamarisk, and everywhere the blue sky caught the earth in pools of blue larkspur."

a wilderness of flowers, and bowers of myrtles, oranges and lemons, smothered with fruits and flowers." Russell's youngest daughter continued to live in the house until the 1850s. In 1857 it became the house of R. F. W. Alston, a prominent planter and governor of South Carolina.

The devastating effects of the Civil War (1861–1865) had a tremendous impact on both city and plantation gardens alike. While many of Charleston's finest plantations, including Middleton and Magnolia, suffered tremendous damage and destruction at the hands of Union troops in 1865, the gardens at both these locations miraculously survived. Following the war, Rev. John Grimke Drayton, whose fortune had been reduced to near poverty, was compelled to sell some 1,500 acres of Magnolia Plantation and to open his beloved gardens to the public as a tourist attraction. The gardens soon obtained national and international acclaim and by 1875 paddleboat steamers were taking visitors up the Ashley River each spring to marvel at the Plantation's brilliant display of wisteria, dogwood, and azaleas in an enchanted woodland setting. The glorious display of azaleas was described in *Harper's Magazine* in 1875 as

> solid masses of blossoms in all shades of red, from palest pink to deepest crimson, and now and then a pure white bush like a bride in her snowy lace. Imagine a long walk with the moss-draped live oaks overhead, fairy lakes and bridges in the distance, and on each side the great fluffy masses of rose and pink and crimson reaching far above your head, thousands upon thousands of blossoms packed close together, with no green to mar the intensity of their color.

Magnolia Garden's fame as a tourist attraction was further enhanced when in 1900 the famous Baedeker's travel guide listed it, along with Niagara

Falls and the Grand Canyon, as one of the three most outstanding tourist attractions in America.

Middleton Place also suffered from economic hard times following the Civil War and soon became a sad and deserted wilderness of tangled honeysuckle, southern smilax, brambles, and yellow jessamine. It was not until the early 1920s that this once lovely garden was transformed to its original beauty through the tenacious efforts of J. J. Pringle Smith, a direct descendant of the Middleton family. With the help of his wife, Heningham Ellett, the garden was restored to its former elegance and was officially opened to the public as a tourist attraction in 1925. Middleton Place received extensive national coverage and within a very short time established itself as a beautiful, cared-for garden offering many themes of contemplation for the public. By 1940 attendance

J. J. Pringle Smith, a Middleton Place descendant, and his wife, Heningham, not only restored Middleton Place to its original glory but also enhanced the setting by planting thirty-five thousand azaleas along the hillside of the Rice Mill Pond.

at the gardens reached 15,000, and in 1941 Middleton Place received the Garden Club of America's coveted Buckley Medal in commemoration of two hundred years of enduring beauty.

Charleston's town gardens were also severely damaged during these turbulent times and afterwards were sorely neglected in order to meet more pressing demands. A northern reporter described Charleston shortly after the Civil War as "a city of ruins, of desolation, of vacant houses, of widowed women, of rotting wharves, of deserted warehouses, of weed filled gardens, of miles of grass grown streets of acres of pitiful and voiceful barrenness." Charleston suffered for many years following the war under what has been appropriately described as genteel poverty, a time that left little in the way of financial resources to keep up with current gardening and horticultural trends. This, no doubt, accounts for the observation by Frances Duncan in *The Century Magazine* that few gardens in Charleston conformed to the Victorian practice of "bedding out" or followed Andrew Jackson Downing's principles of informal design: "Rarely is the serenity of a Charleston garden marred by 'bedding out,' by tightly packed beds of violently diverse colors. . . . Nor is the 'landscape garden' often among those present; that is, the garden which concerns itself chiefly with green lawns and informal shrubbery."

It was not until the early 1900s that a renewed interest in Charleston's town gardens began to emerge. These new gardens were much smaller and more modest in scale than those of the past. Perhaps due to poor economic conditions, or simply because professional garden designers were unavailable during this time, Charleston gardeners began to resort to their own talents to fashion many small creative town gardens. Thus, in the 1920s and 1930s tourists began to visit Charleston not only to see Magnolia and Middleton Gardens, but also to experience the wonderful display of spring flowers in the city's charming town gardens. Marion Cran, an English traveler and author of *Gardens in America*, described several of Charleston's delightful small gardens as they appeared about this time:

> Mrs. Beverley Mikels took care that I saw some of the beautiful little gardens in the town itself—as distinct from the plantation gardens I had been visiting. . . . I have always loved more than size and splendour the evidences of character in gardens. . . . Long observation has taught me to look for it mostly in little gardens; I am accustomed to search diligently in humble places for signs of the authentic poetry of the heart.

> It was there in Mrs. John Simond's garden, fresh, cool and watered, with its wall fountain and pestle bird-bath, a golden arbour of Banksia rose, tulips, bearded irises, snapdragons and stocks; in Mrs. Mikels's own garden where she echoes the purple wisteria in purple iris and stock, and fills her window-boxes now with pansies, and later with clear Rosy Morn petunias to catch the note of a large pink mimosa which blooms in May.

> We saw Mrs. W. B. Ravenel's green lawn and oleanders, Clara Butt tulips, larkspur and madonna lilies in their simple and attractive planting; and Mrs. Geer's overhang of yellow Banksia roses, her ginkgo, weeping almond and wonderful *weigelia rosea*. There was a very fine fig tree which took my eye; and Mrs. Mikels laughed.

> "There is one in every Charleston garden!" she said. "It is a small green sugar fig, the 'celestial' variety."

While most of these newer gardens were contemporary in design, each was endowed with an appealing old-world charm by virtue of their historic setting and wealth of details—high brick walls, iron gateways, spacious piazzas, cobblestone walks, and a myriad of eighteenth- and nineteenth-century architectural details. Margaret Mikell Barnwell (1888–1957), a native of Camden, South Carolina, and a longtime resident of Charleston, designed many of Charleston's city gardens during this period. Barnwell's love of gardening and artistic eye led to her development as a professional garden designer, and in 1928 she began to design, plant, and maintain many of Charleston's local gardens. The first garden Barnwell designed was for Mrs. Andrew J. Geer on Gibbes Street and her final work was the design of the historic Manigault House garden.

The design of Charleston's small town gardens reached a state of refinement under the professional influence of landscape architect Loutrel Briggs (1893–1977). Briggs' involvement in Charleston's garden movement of the 1930s and 1940s, as well as the legacy of gardens he designed in Charleston throughout his career, played an important role in creating a design style that was appropriate to the climate, architecture, historic setting, and lifestyle of the city. Loutrel Briggs, above all others, is credited with establishing the term—Charleston Garden—a descriptive title that has gained national and international recognition and acclaim.

Charleston's gardening activities in the early 1900s were also greatly enhanced through the pioneering efforts of the Garden Club of Charleston, formed in 1922 by a nucleus of ten original members with a common objective to advance gardening in the city. The first civic activity initiated by this visionary group was the planting and caring of the grounds of the Charleston Library Society in 1923. This was followed by an innovative project called the Gateway Walk. Dedicated on 10 April 1930 to celebrate the 250th anniversary of the founding of Charleston, the Gateway Walk was designed to carry visitors through four of the city's oldest churchyards—past ornate monuments, beautiful wrought-iron gates, decorative fences, and ancient live oak trees. Over the years the Gateway Walk has been enjoyed by thousands of tourists. One of the most important projects sponsored by the Garden Club of Charleston was a spring walking tour of private city gardens that are tucked away behind protected walls. Originally designed for the enjoyment and pleasure of its members, the spring garden tour soon developed into a popular tourist attraction featuring the charming town gardens for which Charleston has become so famous. Over time Charleston has become known as an enchanted city of gardens—each year drawing an increasing number of visitors who come to experience the incomparable springtime display and to share in the continuing legacy and tradition of fine gardens, both old and new.

Charleston's Gateway Walk

Beginning on Archdale Street in the churchyards of St. John's Lutheran and the Unitarian churches, the route continues across King Street through the grounds of the Charleston Library Society and the Gibbes Art Gallery, past Meeting Street to the Congregational Church, and finally to the cemetery and churchyard of historic St. Phillip's Episcopal Church.

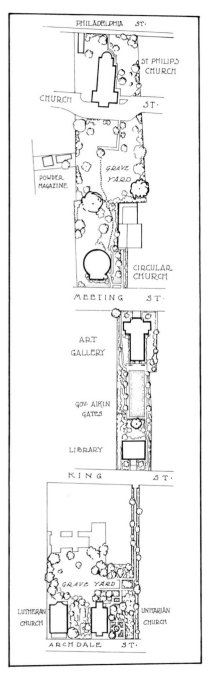

43

Charleston's Garden Setting

The gardens of historic Charleston have few equals in beauty, variety, and old-world charm. In comparison to other American cities, Charleston's town gardens have a distinctive style and setting all their own. The term *Charleston garden* almost universally conveys a visual image of a small private garden enclosed by vine-covered walls and tastefully filled with a profusion of seasonal plants. Wrought-iron gates, old garden walls, antique brick, decorative fountains, statuary, benches, and piazzas are all characteristic features generally associated with a typical Charleston garden. While individual gardens will vary in detail and design, there exists certain base elements inherent to all Charleston gardens—integration of house and garden, maximum use of limited space, enclosure by protective walls, and a creative use of ornamental plants. These features have evolved over time and have been influenced by a variety of factors including climate, architecture, enclosure, and the city's physical plan.

Climate

Perhaps the single most important factor that influenced the historical development of Charleston's gardens was climate. Charleston's semitropical climate is characterized by long, hot summers and relatively mild winters. Even though temperatures occasionally drop below 20°F in winter and rise above 100°F in summer, the average annual temperature for the city is a comfortable 65°F. Charleston lies on latitude 32°N, the same as Bermuda and San Diego, California. The city has a long growing season which extends almost ten months out of the year; the first freeze usually occurs in early December with the last frost by mid-February. Charleston's short winter is traditionally followed by a glorious spring as described by DuBose Heyward, noted Charleston novelist, poet, and playwright:

> Usually by the first of March, the short winter is over and spring pre-empts the city. This is a dramatic invasion, starting with the waxy perfection of the camellia bloom and a spray or two of yellow jessamine. While the nights are still frosty it seems to hang poised and then descends, sweeping the parks and gardens with a tidal wave of color and perfume. Climbing roses foam over old garden walls. Wisteria hangs like purple clouds in ancient pine and oak, and every where the azalea seems to spend itself in a short breathing burst of color.

Charleston's climate is favorably influenced by the fact that the city is bounded by two rivers—the

"Walled gardens, as exemplified in the charming old city of Charleston, South Carolina."

Woman's Home Companion (May 1926)

A typical walled Charleston garden

ABOVE all else, these old Charleston gardens have a marvelous sense of seclusion and privacy. There is also a perfect mergence of house and garden; between these two, it is out in the garden that one reads, plays bridge, sews or has tea inevitably—and invariably. The close proximity of the garden to the house is, of course, what gives this intimate quality, while the wonderful walls—architecturally speaking, the chief glory of the gardens—insure the absolute privacy. These walls are usually solid and seven or eight feet high, so that from the street the only glimpse of the garden is through an exquisite wrought-iron gate, swung between great gateposts, as illustrated here.

Gateway to Stoney House by moonlight

Vista through garden toward wrought-iron gateway

Cooper on the east and the Ashley on the west—and a spacious harbor on the south. While the hot and humid conditions of summer prevail from June through August, temperatures are moderated somewhat by cool ocean breezes from the south and west which are prevalent in late afternoon and early evening. This phenomenon occurs during the summer months when warm air over the land begins to rise and is replaced by cooler ocean air, resulting in refreshing cool breezes which have been described as the number one blessing of Charleston's climate in warm weather. Even with this cooling effect, by early June the heat begins to take its toll and many of the city's inhabitants go off to the beaches, or head to Flat Rock or Cashiers in the North Carolina mountains until October, while those who remain confine their outdoor activities to early morning or late afternoon. Author Robert Molloy, in describing the city, observes that "the heat explains that leisurely way of getting around. After generations of becoming acclimatized to long summers, Charlestonians know better than to be in a hurry." Another important aspect of the city's seasonal trends are the tropical storms or hurricanes that occur in the late summer and early fall. These often produce damaging winds, heavy rainfall, rising tides, and flooding.

Architecture

Charleston's semitropical climate greatly influenced the development of a vernacular style of architecture evidenced in the single house—a long, rectangular, free-standing structure specifically designed to respond to local climatic conditions. The single house was typically built with its gable end facing the street and its rooms strung out in a single line in order to obtain cross ventilation. The first floor of the single house was usually raised several feet above the ground to provide protection against flooding during hurricanes and tropical storms and as a health measure since it was considered undesirable for a house to be built on damp ground.

Porches, locally known as piazzas, were constructed perpendicular to the street along the length of the south or west side of the house. There were usually as many tiers of piazzas as there were building stories. Piazzas serve several functions. During cold weather they provided an ideal spot to enjoy the warmth of sunny days that are so typical of the Lowcountry winter, and in summer they afforded shade and protection from the fierce summer sun, thus preventing the house from becoming unbearable during the heat of the day. In late afternoon and evening piazzas caught the cool, refreshing ocean breezes and became delightful outdoor living spaces. Samuel Gaillard Stoney, in *Charleston: Azaleas and Old Bricks*, appropriately described the Charleston single house as

> simply a hot-weather house that can be used in winter, and no-wise a winter house habitable in summer. Its prime reason for being as it is, is the sacred Charleston wind that every hot afternoon blows up from the southwest across the Ashley River and cools off the town for the evening. Notice and you will realize that the "Charleston" house has been trimmed like a sail whenever it was possible to be square against the course of this most favorable of breezes. And like a proper sail it is designed to catch any other air that might be moving.

It is widely speculated that the concept of the single house was introduced from the West Indies by early English settlers from Barbados and eventually evolved into a building style unique to Charleston in both character and form.

Access from the street into a single house was provided by an outer door that opened onto a piazza, which traditionally overlooked a small side garden. This street door provided both an element of privacy and surprise. The perception on entering was that of going through a traditional door and unexpectedly finding oneself in a garden. The real front door was located in the center of the piazza facing the garden. The piazza functioned as a transitional element between the house and garden which was intimately combined as described by Francis Duncan in *The Century Magazine:*

Located on the south or west side of the house to catch prevailing ocean breezes, piazzas serve as cool, outdoor living spaces overlooking small private gardens.

It is difficult indeed to write of an old Charleston Garden apart from the house, for the two have long been intimates, and the grace of the garden, the fragrance of years of roses, has lent a poignant sweetness to the grave dignity of the mansion, which for more than a century has stretched walls like protecting arms about the gardens loveliness; while the response of the house, born of the rare qualities of nobility of proportion, of harmony, of balance, has dowered the garden with something of its own serenity, its memories, its unvexed quietness.

The piazza also served as an outdoor room from which the side garden could be viewed and enjoyed. Many of Charleston's early gardens were laid out as small patterned gardens which were simple versions of French and English parterres fashionable in Europe during the seventeenth, eighteenth, and nineteenth centuries. The plans of these gardens were based on a combination of geometric shapes including circles, squares, and rectangles which during the Victorian period were often replaced by diamonds, hearts, and stars as well as paisley and floral designs. The shapes of individual beds comprising a pattern garden were interrelated so that they formed a unified pattern or design. In some designs the number of individual beds was small (six, eight, or ten) while in others it was much greater. Beds were usually slightly raised and bordered with boxwood, brick, or sometimes tiles and were planted with old-fashioned annuals, perennials, and flowering bulbs. Paths were made of sandshell, gravel, or tamped or crushed oyster shells. Pleasing views of Charleston's small patterned gardens were afforded from the piazza from which their layout could be easily observed and enjoyed year around.

A Traditional Charleston Entrance

"The street entrance, usually classical and with a fanlight opens onto the end of one of the galleries (piazzas), a gallery so interrelated with the garden that the sensation on entering is that of going through a conventional door and unexpectedly finding oneself in a garden."

John Linley, architectural historian

Enclosure

Another distinctive feature of nearly all gardens in the older sections of Charleston was their containment by high brick or stucco walls. These formidable enclosures were not built originally for aesthetic reasons but, in reality, were constructed to provide protection against intruders. According to Shaffer, in *Carolina Gardens*, the walls insured that household slaves were secured in the confines of the property at night, since a fine would be imposed on the owner if a slave was found in the streets after curfew had sounded. It can certainly be assumed that these protective walls provided privacy which was needed because of the closeness of individual houses and lots. They also helped to contain domestic animals such

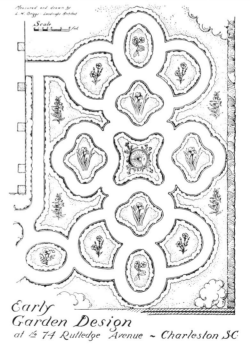

Early
Garden Design
at № 74 Rutledge Avenue ~ Charleston SC.

Laid out in the 1790s, this small patterned garden is believed to be one of the oldest in the city. The garden was originally owned by Peter Bocquet—a Frenchman who exhibited a great interest in plants. Measured and drawn by Loutrel Briggs.

An Old Charleston Wall

Many walls in Charleston contain intricate grillwork, or clairvoyées, which were purely a Dutch invention despite the French name. These openings were designed to permit views and glimpses of gardens hidden behind protected walls. Views of Charleston's small gardens were also made possible by beautifully designed wrought-iron gates. These limited but enticing views of Charleston's gardens are still considered one of the city's greatest delights. Over the years Charleston's garden walls have mellowed with time and are softened by flowering vines and shrubs which provide splashes of color and seasonal charm.

as cows, chickens, and horses which were housed at the rear of many properties up until the latter part of the nineteenth century.

Over time these protective walls took on a more decorative character and became an integral part of a garden's overall design. Beautifully designed, they were frequently constructed of brick or tabby—a mixture consisting of oyster shells and lime. Many of these early walls incorporated fanciful arches covered with stucco in soft pastel colors of light green, blue, peach, ochre, and yellow, reflecting a strong influence of early settlers from the West Indies. The color of stucco was determined by the addition of natural pigments or the application of color washes. The extensive use of stucco on Charleston buildings

and garden walls during the eighteenth and nineteenth centuries resulted from European customs and architectural styles.

City Plan

Another factor which greatly influenced the evolution of Charleston's single house and integrated garden plan was the development of the city's overall plan. With limited area in which to expand, high land costs, and the development of a multidirectional street layout, a very compact city plan evolved, as confirmed by the Reverend Mr. Hewat in a description of the city in 1779: "the streets from east to west extend from river to river. . . . These streets are

A fanciful iron grille, or clairvoyée, provides an enticing view of a walled garden on Lamboll Street.

intersected by others, nearly at right angles, and throw the town into a number of squares with dwelling houses on the front and offices, houses (dependencies) and little gardens behind." To accommodate the physical restrictions imposed by this layout, land lots were generally long and narrow, with few being serviced by alleys or public easements to take care of access to stables, servant quarters, detached kitchens, and working yards that were an integral part of Charleston households. It can be surmised that this dense living arrangement was acceptable in part since Charleston inhabitants had come from European cities where conditions were crowded and houses were traditionally built close together. As noted by architectural historian Kenneth Severens in *Charleston—Antebellum Architecture and Civic Destiny*, "the single house offered a masterful but still vernacular solution to the residential problems of comfort, privacy and propriety. Single houses were sensitive compromises between the public need for urban density and the private desire for domestic seclusion."

The rectangular shape of the single house not only appropriately responded to Charleston's climatic conditions but also readily fit into the space allotted

On viewing Charleston from the balcony of St. Michael's Church in the spring of 1791, George Washington provided a description of the city that, over time, has remained virtually unchanged: "the whole is seen in one view, and to advantage, the Gardens and green trees which are interspersed add much to the beauty of the prospect" (Washington's diary, 7 May 1791).

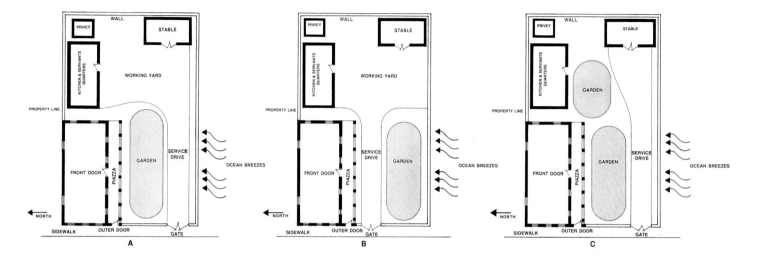

Plans A and B depict typical layouts of Charleston house and garden plans. Plan C shows an expansion of the side garden to the rear of the property. This transition occurred during the early part of the twentieth century as the need for service yards gradually disappeared.

by the city's dense urban plan. To maximize the layout, the long side of the house opposite the piazza was generally located directly on the lot line at the northern or eastern corner of the property in order to provide adequate space for domestic service needs. This arrangement provided space for a small side garden and service drive plus ample room at the rear of the property for slave quarters, kitchen, carriage house, stables, privy, and well.

By the early part of the twentieth century the need for servants quarters, stables, carriage houses, and other utilitarian elements had all but disappeared, thus allowing the typical side garden to be expanded to the rear of the property. Over the years there developed many variations of this layout due to differences in lot sizes, architectural diversity, and building configurations, but as a general rule tremendous consistency has prevailed in the traditional arrangement of the overall house and garden plan.

In contrast to Charleston's traditional layout of house and garden plan, in nearby Savannah an arrangement developed which was distinctly different in overall form. Similar to Charleston in the development of many long, narrow residential lots, the one important difference in Savannah's city plan was the placement of central alleys, referred to locally as lanes, that extended down the middle of its residential blocks. These public easements permitted the building of traditional town houses which could be positioned on the site with their front facades close to the street and ample space remaining at the back for a porch and small garden. Outbuildings and servants quarters were also placed at the rear of the property with service access being provided by the alley behind. Architectural historian John Linley speculates in *Georgia Landscape* that

> had Charleston been laid out according to the Savannah plan, the typical Charleston house would likely have been a row house. Those facing south, like those facing South Battery and the park (White Point Garden) at the tip of the peninsular, would doubtless have had the garden and porches in front; those facing north, like

those in Savannah, would likely have had the porches and gardens in the rear. Instead, old Charleston houses appear to be completely unconventional. Tall and narrow, partly classical and partly vernacular with porches that seem more of the garden than of the house.

These contrasting site layouts are responsible for the hidden gardens of Savannah that are located at the rear of the property and thus secluded from view, and the private gardens of Charleston which can be seen, or at least partially viewed, from the street. It is this public exposure of small, side gardens that gives Charleston the impression of being a city set in a garden. Charleston gardens serve as personal contributions to the overall beauty of the town and are as integral a part of the fabric of the city as the houses which they embrace.

A View of Savannah in 1837 by Firmin Cerveau (1812–1896)

Based on a plan prepared by James Edward Oglethorpe, the city was beautifully laid out in wards, tithings, and public squares. Residential blocks were arranged with row houses, service alleys, and rear porches overlooking small private gardens.

Loutrel Briggs and Charleston's Garden Style

Charleston's garden style, as it is known today, was greatly influenced by the eminent landscape architect Loutrel W. Briggs (1893–1977). Loutrel Briggs not only designed many of Charleston's small private gardens but also the grounds and gardens of numerous Lowcountry plantations. Through his versatile talents as a designer, writer, and garden historian, Briggs played an important and significant role in refining Charleston's garden style and in preserving and documenting Charleston's garden history. His legacy lives today in many fine city and plantation gardens and through his research and writing contained in his book, *Charleston Gardens*.

Loutrel Winslow Briggs was born 12 December 1893 in New York City to Frank E. and Ella Loutrel Briggs. After graduating from Cornell University in 1917 with a degree in rural art (landscape architecture), he became head of the Department of Landscape Architecture at the New York School of Fine and Applied Art. In 1921 Briggs opened an independent practice of landscape architecture in New York City. His talent for garden design was recognized early in his career. In 1924 he won first place for a garden entry he sponsored in New York's International Flower Show and as a prize was allowed to travel and photograph gardens in Italy, France, and England. Upon returning from this European tour, Briggs gave illustrated lectures on European gardens at the Metropolitan Museum of Art, the International Garden Club, the Horticultural Society of New York, and other east coast clubs and organizations. The opportunity to visit and study the great gardens of Europe was to have a profound influence on his sensitivity to and interest in garden design and history.

Loutrel Briggs first visited Charleston in 1927. Like many other visitors during this time he did not come as a tourist in the traditional sense but as a winter resident taking up lodging for the season in one of the city's small inns or old hotels. Thereafter, Briggs returned each winter, frequently residing at the Brewton Inn located at the corner of Church and Tradd Street, until he became a permanent resident of the city in 1959. In addition to his landscape architecture practice in New York, Briggs also opened a Charleston office in 1929. This was the beginning of his system of practicing landscape architecture in the north during the summer and in Charleston during the winter. Work in his New York office included projects in New York, New Jersey, Pennsylvania, and New England. It was through his New York office that Loutrel Briggs' early commissions in Charleston would develop. As Northerners began to purchase historic Charleston houses and Lowcountry plantations as winter retreats during the 1920s and

The Reserve in Summer
by Alice Ravenel Huger Smith
(watercolor on paper)

Along with other artists in the 1920s and 1930s, Alice Ravenel Huger Smith helped create a greater awareness of the beauty of Charleston and the Carolina Lowcountry. Loutrel Briggs also played an important role in this effort through his many articles on Charleston's city and plantation gardens as well as his contributions to the art of garden design.

1930s, they often sought the professional services of a recognized landscape architect in the north to assist with the design of gardens and grounds of these properties. It can be assumed that these early commissions in part led to Briggs' initial visits to Charleston in order to collaborate with clients on various landscape projects.

At the time Loutrel Briggs arrived in Charleston, the city was undergoing a cultural renaissance in art, literature, music, and drama. Beginning in the 1920s and lasting well into the 1930s, this dynamic movement led to a greater appreciation of Charleston's physical beauty and cultural past. Charleston's cultural revival was dominated by a small but creative group of artists and writers, including Alfred Hutty, Alice Ravenel Huger Smith, Anna Heyward Taylor, Elizabeth O'Neill Verner, Josephine Pinckney, and DuBose Heyward. Although each came from different backgrounds and training, they collectively formed a vibrant artistic community that played an important role in redefining Charleston's cultural heritage and in kindling a new appreciation of the unique physical and visual environment of the Carolina Lowcountry. Loutrel Briggs soon contributed to this flourishing artistic movement through his articles on Charleston's gardens and his legacy to the art of garden design.

One of Loutrel Briggs' first commissions in Charleston was in 1929 for Mrs. Washington Roebling, widow of the famous engineer who designed the Brooklyn Bridge. After acquiring the historic William Gibbes House on South Battery, Mrs. Roebling was eager to create a new garden but was insistent that it be done in the spirit of the past. Briggs' design was based on remnants of an earlier garden that had existed on the site and on the historic tradition of other Charleston gardens. Featured in the

March 1933 issue of *House and Garden,* the Roebling garden beautifully illustrated Loutrel Briggs' sensitivity for design within the framework of a historic setting. In addition to this early commission for Mrs. Roebling, Briggs soon became actively involved in the design of gardens and grounds for numerous Lowcountry estates and plantations. Plantation gardens designed by Loutrel Briggs, included among others, Mulberry for Mr. and Mrs. Clarence Chapman of New York (1930), Rice Hope for Senator J. S. Freulinghuysen of New Jersey (1932), and Mepkin for Henry and Clare Booth Luce (1937). On seeing the gardens created by Loutrel Briggs at Mulberry, E. T. H. Shaffer in *Carolina Gardens* wrote: "For romantic story, beauty of location, sympathy and perfection in execution, I have found no finer garden anywhere than at Mulberry-on-Cooper."

In addition to his active landscape architectural practices in New York and Charleston, Briggs frequently lectured to garden clubs, horticultural societies, museums, and civic organizations. He also found time to write numerous articles, many of which appeared to be on his favorite subject—Charleston gardens. Prior to his article on the Roebling garden in 1933, Briggs had written an article for *Country Life* in 1930 entitled "Amateur Gardens—As Seen by a Landscape Architect." This essay provided an interesting look at the work of amateur designers and highlighted three Charleston gardens, including those of Mrs. A. J. Geer, Mrs. J. C. Simonds, and Elizabeth O'Neill Verner, a local Charleston artist. Briggs considered each of these gardens to be excellent examples of amateur work. Additional articles entitled "Little Patterned Gardens of Charleston" (1934) and "Charleston's Famous Gardens" (1939) appeared in *House and Garden* magazine. Loutrel

William Gibbes House Garden

One of Loutrel Briggs' first commissions in Charleston was to design a garden for the historic William Gibbes House for Mrs. Washington Roebling. The illustrations show the formal garden and reflecting pool (below) and a view of the terrace and outbuildings sheltered beneath a canopy of live oak trees (left).

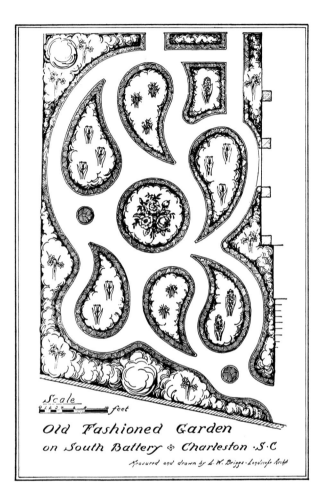

Scale ___feet

Old Fashioned Garden

on South Battery ✧ Charleston ·S·C

Measured and drawn by L. W. Briggs · Landscape Archt.

The William Washington House Garden

A plan of the William Washington House garden as measured and drawn by Loutrel Briggs (above) and a photograph of the garden as it exists today (facing page). Briggs documented the history of many of Charleston's city and plantation gardens in his book *Charleston Gardens.*

Briggs is best known for his book *Charleston Gardens,* published in 1951. This comprehensive work, which included over twenty years of research, documented the history of Charleston gardens and provided illustrated accounts of city and plantation gardens. The book's primary purpose, as described by Briggs, was to educate and enlighten by depicting and illustrating the magic and charm of Charleston gardens. In so doing, it would encourage others to apply the same ideas and design principles to their own gardens in the hope of bringing greater enjoyment and beauty to other places.

Throughout his career Briggs demonstrated an exceptional ability to handle a variety of landscape architectural projects encompassing a wide range of commercial, institutional, governmental, and residential designs. Representative project types included school grounds, government housing, college campuses, church grounds, cemeteries, suburban estates, plantations, and many small city gardens. In 1941 the Carolina Art Association sponsored an exhibition at the Gibbes Art Gallery of some thirty drawings, photographs, and paintings illustrating the gardens and grounds designed by Briggs in both the north and south. The exhibition also included a series of measured drawings prepared by Briggs of old gardens that still existed in Charleston at the time.

Loutrel Briggs gave freely of his time and talents to assist with many worthwhile cultural and civic projects including Charleston's Gateway Walk, the restoration of many of Charleston's historic gardens, and design of the South Carolina Memorial Garden honoring those who served in World War II. Additionally, he sought to educate and instill in others an understanding and love of gardens and garden design. As early as 1928 Briggs spoke to the Garden Club of Charleston on "The ABC's of Garden

Design," and frequently presented study courses covering such topics as general principles of garden design, identification of southern flora, and field lectures on Charleston garden plants. Briggs' own private garden on Ladson Street in Charleston's historic district was often included among those open to the public each spring in an effort to foster an interest in gardening and to raise funds for many local preservation and beautification efforts.

Of all his projects, Briggs appears to have gained greatest satisfaction and pride from his small garden designs. Within Charleston alone he designed more than a hundred small gardens, many of which are still treasured today for their unique and individual charm. In designing Charleston's small gardens, Briggs adhered to certain basic design principles that proved to be of tremendous benefit throughout his career. He believed that each space and its surroundings should be carefully considered in determining the design of an individual garden. Another important principle was that, if at all possible, the garden should be visible and easily accessible from the house to establish a close interior/exterior relationship between the house and garden plan. His desire was to create a garden that was an outdoor room. Briggs also placed great importance on understanding the needs and desires of his clients. His ultimate objective was to create gardens that would bring continued pleasure and enjoyment to their owners and to develop creative and workable design solutions that would satisfy their individual needs. Briggs obviously was successful in this endeavor for many of his clients became lifelong friends, frequently commissioning him to update an original design or to design a new garden when a move was made to a different location.

Briggs exhibited a marvelous talent for garden design. This is evidenced in the many small and delightful gardens he designed in Charleston's historic district. Design for these small gardens presented many challenges due to their odd and erratic shapes and the physical constraints imposed by shade, access, and architectural demands. Briggs possessed an unusual talent to work within the constraints of these tiny spaces and to fashion many creative and artistic designs.

A particular trademark of a Briggs' garden was the sensitive use of appropriate plants. Briggs believed that each plant should be selected based on its individual character and ability to perform within the limitations of space. As a general rule he relied on a restricted palette of twenty-five or thirty traditional Charleston plants. Plants commonly used by Briggs included the camellia, azalea, loquat, tea olive, wisteria, yellow jessamine, oleander, and star jasmine. Briggs' limited use of traditional plants not only helped to unify the garden's design but also provided a strong and continuous link with the past. In many cases Briggs incorporated into his designs a beautiful stretch of lawn or a flower border planted with perennials, annuals, and bulbs.

In addition to his sensitive use of plants, Briggs also relied on the use of traditional building materials such as old Charleston bricks and antique stone in the construction of walls, walks, steps, terraces, patios, pools, and edgings. The appropriate use of these authentic materials helped to articulate and enhance his designs and to relate the garden and house to their surroundings. Selection and placement of garden features including sculpture, decorative pots, urns, benches, arbors, and gates were important features of a Briggs' garden and were used to add interest and appeal to the overall design. These were often placed at the end of an axis or served as the central focal point of the garden. It was Loutrel

A Briggs Garden in Spring

Loutrel Briggs exhibited a marvelous talent for working within the constraints of Charleston's confined urban spaces to create many beautiful and imaginative garden designs.

Briggs, above all others, who was credited with introducing into Charleston's eighteenth- and nineteenth-century architectural settings a distinctive garden style that has prevailed throughout the twentieth century.

Ownership of a Briggs garden has become a Charleston tradition and has been compared to owning something bearing the English Hallmark, or a piece of silver marked sterling. Loutrel Briggs will live in the hearts and minds of all who have seen and experienced the beauty of a Charleston garden in spring or who share in his belief of the privilege that is ours to enjoy the beauty and wonders of nature.

A Gardener's Garden

Emily Whaley's garden is a small secluded garden located on Church Street in Charleston's historic district. The design of the garden is based on a plan prepared by Loutrel Briggs in 1942. The garden contains three distinct areas or garden rooms designed around a circular motif—each with its own individual character and charm. Entrance to the garden is obtained through a decorative wrought-iron gate that opens onto a winding flagstone path filled with a variety of shade-loving plants—camellias, azaleas, loquats (*Eriobotrya japonica*), podocarpus, holly fern (*Cyrtomium falcatum*), Japanese box, and fatsia (*Fatsia japonica*). The path continues to a small terrace and enclosed service area located adjacent to the rear of the house. Views along the path create a feeling of anticipation and discovery of the garden beyond.

The garden is symmetrical in design and extends along a central axis to a brick carriage house at the extremity of the property. The initial garden room is elliptical in shape—the central portion of which is planted in grass and flanked by borders filled with lush plantings of annuals, perennials, and flowering shrubs. Old Charleston bricks are used to create borders between the lawn area and the planting beds and to articulate and define the garden's design.

Typical plantings within the borders include tulips, iris, jonquils, stock, snapdragons, and pansies in spring, followed by summer plantings of blue salvia, alyssum, begonias, geraniums, impatiens, verbena, phlox, lantana, dahlias, nicotiana, and plumbago. Roses, star jasmine, and other vines are planted on fences which separate the garden from neighboring properties.

The second garden room is circular in design, planted with grass and enclosed with plantings of Japanese box (*Buxus microphylla* var. *japonica*),

Originally planned as a spring garden, in recent years it has been planted with annuals, perennials, and flowering shrubs to extend its blooming period into late May and early June.

A view of the garden in spring. The garden has a feeling of
spaciousness that belies the fact that it is contained within a
long, narrow space less than 30 feet wide and 150 feet long.

pittosporum (*Pittosporum tobira*), azaleas, and camellias. This area is also defined with a border of old Charleston brick which provides definition to the design and adds a feeling of age to the garden. A small circular pool, only 1½ inches deep, is located in the lawn along the central axis of the garden. The pool serves as a major focal point and a magnet for birds. The pool's mirror-like surface reflects the colors of surrounding plants and flowers.

Low pierced brick walls and columns, placed perpendicular to the main axis of the garden, are located between the second and third garden rooms. These low garden walls serve as transition elements between the two formal, sunny areas of the garden and the remaining garden room which is more informal and shaded. This final space is paved with brick and surrounded by plantings of azaleas, camellias, and hydrangeas as well as ferns, wild flowers, and other shade-loving plants. A spreading live oak from a neighboring property provides a

canopy of green. A small pool and several decorative garden benches add a sense of tranquility to this natural setting.

The garden contains a number of decorative features and furnishings—a white scalloped fence provides privacy; sculptured figures add interest and accent; garden benches and seats provide the opportunity for relaxation and enjoyment; and decorative urns, pots, and containers planted with annuals provide seasonal color and charm.

The enchantment of this elegant town garden is a result of its imaginative design and the creative plant compositions fashioned by the hands of its owner, Emily Whaley. While the basic design of the garden has remained constant over the years, plantings within the garden have changed as Ms. Whaley has experimented with various plant arrangements and color combinations. Described by English garden writer, Rosemary Verey, as a dream garden and featured in such notable publications as *The American Woman's Garden* and Caroline Boissett's *Town Gardens*, Emily Whaley's garden has gained international recognition as a classic Charleston garden.

A Garden Retreat

Located off Meeting Street in the heart of Charleston's historic district, this small urban garden was designed by Loutrel Briggs for Mr. and Mrs. James Hagood in 1969. This was the second garden Briggs had designed for the Hagoods, the first being a much larger garden on Legare Street in 1947. Briggs was often retained by clients to design a second garden when a new house was purchased or when revisions to an existing garden were desired.

The Meeting Street garden occupies a small rectangular space no larger than 45 feet by 50 feet on

An assortment of garden furnishings and accessories has been carefully selected and placed in the garden to add interest and complement the overall design.

This delightful walled garden represents a wonderful blend of natural and hardscape features. The generous use of brick and flagstone helps to define individual garden spaces and assists in reducing ongoing maintenance.

From the entrance gate the eye is drawn into the garden by a series of focal points which articulate and enhance the overall design.

which once stood several brick outbuildings and two large trees. In order to make room for the garden and obtain adequate light, the existing structures were demolished and one of the trees removed. The garden is divided into two separate areas, or outdoor rooms. Each is designed on a different level to accommodate a slight change of grade and to add interest and visual appeal. The first garden room consists of a small paved terrace enclosed by a brick wall softened by a mixed planting of ornamental shrubs and several small trees. A circular pool originally served as the focal point of the garden but was later replaced with a decorative piece of sculpture bordered by Japanese box (*Buxus microphylla* var. *japonica*). Adjoining the terrace is a small greenhouse with sitting room that contains many unusual and exotic plants, a stone fountain, and a pool.

The second garden room is based on a motif that consists of brick paving in a circular design. An antique sundial serves as the central feature of the design. Enclosed by a pierced brick wall, the garden is planted with azaleas, camellias, and a variety of seasonal plants. Japanese box is repeated as a border planting to provide continuity and to articulate the design.

This delightful garden, while relatively new in comparison to other Charleston gardens, is so well conceived in its traditional use of paving materials, plants, and garden features that it has the look and feel of a much older garden. Over the years the garden has been beautifully preserved in its original design.

An antique sundial serves as the central element of this small garden room.

A Spring Garden

Located on the lower end of King Street just around the corner from White Point Garden, this small gem of a garden was designed by Loutrel Briggs for Mr. and Mrs. Lloyd Willcox in 1951. Protected behind high brick walls, the garden is entered through a decorative wrought-iron gate that, as a rule, is always open during spring when the garden is in full bloom.

Once inside the garden the eye is drawn to a shaded path extending along the side of the house to a rear entrance and arched stucco wall which serves as an interesting focal point and backdrop for garden ornaments and pots of seasonal plants. To the left of the garden gate lies a flagstone walk that leads to the main entrance of the house past a small colorful garden divided into a series of perfectly proportioned outdoor rooms. Each room is defined by a low brick wall or a clipped hedge of Japanese box (*Buxus microphylla* var. *japonica*). Slight changes of elevation in the garden create a feeling of spaciousness and add interest to the overall design.

A small covered porch located along the front of the house provides an ideal spot from which the garden can be seen and enjoyed. The porch is attractively furnished with many colorful pots of geraniums in spring and hanging baskets filled with begonias and impatiens in summer. A small seating area located in the front corner of the garden under the spreading canopy of a large hackberry tree (*Celtis laevigata*) is an ideal location to catch the warm morning sun and to gain a different perspective of the garden as it changes with the light during the course of the day.

The walls surrounding the garden are softened with ivy and plantings of azaleas, camellias, aucuba, and nandinas. Lush plantings of cleyera (*Cleyera japonica*), fatshedera (*Fatshedera lizei*), podocarpus (*Podocarpus macrophyllus*), and holly fern (*Cyrtomium falcatum*) add seasonal interest and a finished look to the design. In spring the garden is filled with bulbs and annuals to create a striking display of color and form. Several garden features, including a dolphin fountain and lion's head ornament, add visual interest and personal charm.

Protected behind high walls, this gem of a garden is divided into a series of perfectly proportioned outdoor rooms. Garden walls are softened with plantings of ivy, azaleas, camellias, and other ornamental shrubs. A small birdbath and statue of St. Francis serve as the focal point of the main garden room.

Charleston's Small Town Gardens

There is a charm and beauty about Charleston's small gardens that once experienced is not easily forgotten. Secluded behind antique walls in picturesque eighteenth- and nineteenth-century architectural settings, the small gardens of Charleston serve as hidden sanctuaries and private retreats. The enchantment of these small peaceful gardens is found in the beauty of wrought-iron gates, fine doorways, elegant columns, old walls, distinctive piazzas, and an endless array of colorful and sweet-scented plants.

Charleston's small town gardens require skillful planning and design to achieve pleasing compositions that appropriately fit within the city's dense urban spaces formed by narrow lots, high walls, and a variety of old and historic structures. Within these limited spaces are many creative and imaginative small gardens fashioned to reflect a feeling of spaciousness and a harmonious sense of scale. Noted English gardener Rosemary Verey, in writing about "The Walled Gardens of Charleston," describes the challenges facing a designer in creating a beautiful garden in such limited space:

> A designer may find it easy to fashion a landscape with long vistas and a variety of elements, but being confined by space demands a strength of discipline, the ability to see from all angles, to appreciate in all directions, to create a picture within the smallest and most unpropitious corner. . . . The designer has the luxury of using jewels so small and precious that they would be overwhelmed and lost in a larger, more spacious setting. He must be conscious of a feeling of intimacy, remembering how the garden will be seen from the windows and by visitors as they arrive. He must study the reflections, the shafts of light at each hour of the day and each season. There must be a feeling of peace, of interest in every mood, but dominating all there must be the essence of tranquility, no agitation or urge to move on. It should inspire in the beholder a sense of completion and satisfaction.

Charleston's small gardens comprise a series of inviting spaces or outdoor rooms perfectly suited to the climate, culture, and lifestyle of the city. They reflect a wonderful sense of scale achieved by combining house and garden into a unified whole. While they are secluded and private, they are at the same time an integral part of the entire urban scene. Much of their charm and appeal is created by the enticing but limited views they afford from the street through decorative wrought-iron gates as well as the visual benefits they derive from surrounding vistas of

In Charleston's limited garden spaces—where scale is critical and every detail counts—design solutions must be tailored to the constraints and potential of each individual site.

church spires, colorful tiled roofs, picturesque buildings, and ancient walls of neighboring gardens. These delightful urban gardens can best be described as a total sensory experience. Within their intimate spaces one feels the element of age and an appropriate sense of scale; sees the sensitive use of materials and the beauty of line, color, and form; smells the perfume of flowers and the fragrance of sweet-scented vines; and hears the distant chimes of church bells as well as the occasional sounds of silence captured within a totally private world.

Many of Charleston's small gardens are made to feel larger than their actual size through a deceptive use of space. This is achieved through spatial illu-

71

With an increased interest in small space gardening, Charleston's small town gardens provide a wonderful source of inspiration and ideas for anyone planning to create or improve a garden that has limited space.

sions created by the reflective surface of water, subtle changes in elevation, cleverly concealed mirrors, decorative latticework, diminishing perspective, and the imaginative use and placement of plants. They are also greatly embellished with an assortment of ornamental features of appropriate scales and styles. Urns, planters, fountains, sculpture, seats, and benches are but a few of the garden features which add interest and charm.

Plants are one of the greatest joys and pleasures of Charleston's small gardens. They cloth high walls with a mantle of soothing green and provide color, fragrance, and visual interest throughout the year. While attractive at any season, these small gardens are at their finest from mid-March through April when they are filled with the waxy blossoms of camellias; brilliant azaleas; magnificent displays of wisteria, yellow jessamine, Lady Banksia rose; and the delicate greens of holly fern, Japanese box, podocarpus, and fig vine. This magnificent spring time display continues into May and early June with jasmine, magnolias, and oleanders in vivid hues of rose, pink, and red. Even as late spring fades into summer and the days grow long and the humidity rises, Charleston's floral season lingers with the bright colors of vitex, crape myrtle, trumpet vine, althaea, and the exotic fragrance of ginger lilies that lasts well into the fall. The city's short and mild winter, characterized by many warm and sun-filled days, is soon followed in late January with a colorful display of camellias, pansies, narcissus, and daffodils that serve as harbingers of another glorious spring.

Often described as the living essence of a garden, fragrance is one of the most lasting and memorable features of Charleston's small gardens. At almost any season of the year, one can experience the delicate fragrance of flowers, shrubs, and cascading vines, including such treasured favorites as the sweet scent of tea olive (*Osmanthus fragrans*), the alluring delicacy of star jasmine (*Trachelospermum jasminoides*), the penetrating perfume of wisteria (*Wisteria sinensis*), the heavy sweetness of gardenia (*Gardenia jasminoides*), the penetrating fragrance of pittosporum (*Pittosporum tobira*), and the elusive aroma of magnolia (*Magnolia grandiflora*).

Much is to be gained from the experience and lessons in ingenuity represented in Charleston's small gardens for it is here that small space gardening has reached its highest state of refinement. While a garden need not be large to be satisfying, careful planning and design must be completed to achieve its fullest enjoyment by combining pleasing spatial relationships, artistically arranged plants, and hardscape elements into a harmonious and unified whole. The possibilities of design, as exemplified by Charleston's small gardens, are infinite—presenting an endless opportunity to fashion one's own private world in response to climate, culture, site, budget, and personal taste. Whatever the design a small garden may take, it can benefit from the lasting and endearing qualities traditional to Charleston's small space gardens—privacy, serenity, enclosure, fragrance, intimacy, beauty, practicality, and genius for detail.

The creative use of plants is one of the most interesting and striking features of Charleston's small town gardens.

One of the greatest advantages of a small garden is the opportunity to concentrate one's efforts in a limited space to achieve maximum results.

A view through the entrance gate of the Benjamin Phillips House garden. The terrace in the foreground is paved in old Charleston brick and serves as an ideal space for outdoor gatherings.

The Benjamin Phillips House Garden

When the present owners purchased the historic Benjamin Phillips House (ca. 1818) on Church Street in 1987 there was no garden—only concrete paving, a chain link fence, and an unattractive view of several adjoining properties. With the help of Charleston landscape architects Hugh and Mary Palmer Dargan, the site was transformed into an award-winning design featuring a re-created small formal garden. Not only is the resulting garden ideally suited to the lifestyle and desires of its owners but is also a complement to the urban fabric of historic Church Street, a treasure trove of eighteenth- and nineteenth-century architecture.

Access to the garden is gained through a handsome wooden gate that opens onto an attractive garden lane, paved in old Charleston brick. The lane is flanked by evergreen plantings of white anise (*Illicium floridanum* var. *alba*) and espaliered sasanquas (*Camellia sasanqua*) which are underplanted with pansies in winter and impatiens in summer. A second smaller gate, located at the end of the drive, leads to a path that winds past a spacious brick terrace into an elegant walled garden of symmetrical paths and formal beds.

The plan of the re-created formal garden is based on a design frequently found in Charleston in the late eighteenth century. Its layout consists of four square patterns with a circle as a central motif. Planting beds are bordered with antique, oversized brick and edged with Kingsville box (*Buxus microphylla* var. *Kingsville*), selected for its slow growth and diminutive leaf size. Walks are made of sandshell, a material comprised of sand and small ocean shells, frequently used in early Charleston gardens. Heirloom specimens of *Camellia japonica* var. *Debutante,* an old-time favorite, were used to give the garden a feeling of age.

A view of the garden looking toward the house reveals a formal pattern reminiscent of a late eighteenth-century Charleston garden design. The use of heirloom camellias, azaleas, and box for edging adds age and authenticity to the garden's historic character.

Twin, brick garden houses modeled after early Charleston privies, complete with clay tile roofs, are located in opposite corners at the back of the garden. These decorative but utilitarian structures provide space for storage and garden supplies. Nestled between the garden houses are two Hume hollies (*Ilex x attenuata* var. *Hume*) and a small seating area that is a perfect spot to pause and enjoy the beauty of the garden.

To provide privacy the garden is enclosed by high brick walls. These are softened by plantings of several fast-growing vines including akebia (*Akebia quinata*) and star jasmine (*Trachelospermum jasminoides*). A small fountain, antique sundial, and custom-made furniture complement the garden and add interest and charm.

The garden contains twin dependencies complete with antique clay tile roofs. These handsome brick structures serve as ideal locations to store garden equipment and supplies.

The William Pritchard Dove House Garden

The garden of the William Pritchard House (ca. 1816) consists of a space no more than 20 feet wide and 50 feet long. Protected from view along the street by a pierced brick wall, access to the garden is gained along a landscaped lane that doubles as an attractive entrance walk and an area for off-street parking. Designed by Mr. and Mrs. Robert Whitelaw almost thirty years ago, the garden consists of a decorative brick terrace and an elevated panel of emerald green grass, enclosed by an adjoining building at the rear of the property and by decorative garden walls on two sides. The terrace and walls are constructed of brick made by Mr. Whitelaw in the traditional Charleston manner—hand-molded, sun-dried, and fired in a wood-burning kiln. A small porch overlooks the garden and provides a convenient space from which the garden can be enjoyed year around.

This tiny jewel of a garden is at its best in early spring when it is filled with the colorful blossoms of camellias, azaleas, and bright pink tulips carefully

The entrance to the William Pritchard Dove House opens onto a landscaped lane that doubles as an attractive garden walk and an area for off-street parking. The doorway is enhanced with a planting of star jasmine (*Trachelospermum jasminoides*) which provides a profusion of fragrant flowers in late spring and a garland of evergreen foliage throughout the remainder of the year.

A small seventeenth-century Japanese Buddha statue and two antique stone finials serve as handsome garden features.

While essentially a spring garden, the use of evergreens, a carpet of green grass, and a variety of accessories transforms the garden into an outdoor room, enjoyable year-round.

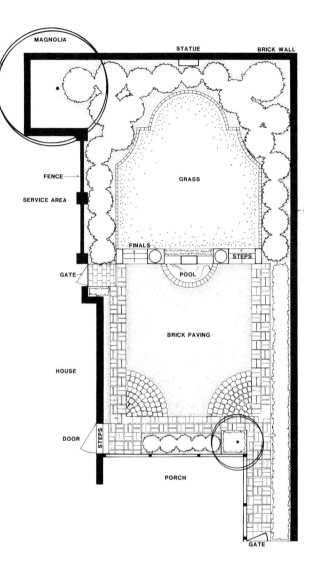

William Pritchard Dove House Garden Plan

selected to create a harmonious color scheme. While the garden is at its peak in early spring, its strong and elegant design—combined with the contrasting texture of ivy (*Hedera helix*), yew (*Podocarpus macrophylla*), and several broadleaf evergreens—provides visual interest throughout the year. Seasonal color is added through the use of pots of annuals placed on the terrace and around the pool during spring, summer, and fall.

This delightful small garden contains several interesting and unique garden features that add visual interest and charm. These include a small pool and fountain, a seventeenth-century Japanese statue that once belonged to the Charleston novelist Josephine Pinckney, and two stone finials rescued from the Exchange Building following the great earthquake of 1886. Another interesting feature is a balustrade wall that separates the garden from a service yard. The balustrades were secured from the wreckage of an abandoned house and have been incorporated into an attractive garden wall.

79

Andrew Hasell House Garden

The Andrew Hasell House was built around 1789 and is an excellent example of a typical single house—many of which were built in Charleston during the economic recovery following the Revolutionary War. The garden of this historic house gives dramatic evidence of what can be accomplished in the awkward confines of a long narrow lot, a feature common to many of the older residential sections of the city. Typical of many single houses, access to the garden is gained by way of a handsome doorway that opens from the street onto an elevated piazza overlooking a small intimate garden. The garden is enclosed on three sides by brick walls which minimize climatic extremes and help create a wonderful private retreat.

This garden was designed in 1952 by the late Margaret Mikell Barnwell (1888–1957), a Charleston resident and talented landscape designer. Many of Barnwell's gardens are pictured in *Charleston Gardens* by Loutrel Briggs. Barnwell's design for the Andrew Hasell House garden maximizes the use of limited space and serves as an excellent example of the integration of house and garden plan. The design of the garden is a skillful composition of open lawn, flagstone terrace, formal beds bordered in old Charleston brick, and walks of sandshell. One of the most outstanding features of the garden is its old-world charm and the graciousness that age lends to its many fine features.

Interest and variety are provided by a richness of plants including tea olives (*Osmanthus fragrans*), camellias, azaleas, box, maidenhair ferns (*Adiantum capillus-veneris*), magnolias, and a magnificent crape myrtle tree (*Lagerstroemia indica*). Color is provided by lush plantings of pansies and English daisies in winter and spring followed by begonias in summer. A small sculpture serves as the garden's focal point and helps to add an appropriate sense of scale. Pots with seasonal plantings provide interest and an opportunity to enhance and expand the overall landscape scheme.

The Andrew Hasell House garden on a misty spring morning. The charm of the garden lies in its richness of plants, beautifully displayed in a lovely eighteenth-century architectural setting.

A view looking north across an emerald green lawn toward a raised piazza that overlooks a traditional side garden.

A small statue encircled with a colorful planting of summer annuals serves as the central feature of the garden.

Coker Garden

The Coker garden is located on Laurens Street in Charleston's historic Ansonborough area. Extensive damage to the original garden by Hurricane Hugo in 1989, including the loss of several large canopy trees, created a unique opportunity to fashion a new garden that is a wonderful blend of both traditional and contemporary designs.

Access to the garden is gained by way of a decorative wrought-iron entrance gate that opens onto a long shaded path lined with a variety of ferns and other shade-loving plants. The central feature of this exciting new garden, designed by Hugh Dargan Associates, is an oval stretch of lawn that serves as the centerpiece for a colorful border of spring and summer flowering plants. Inspired by a love of English gardens, the owners were eager to create a flower border that would last well past the blooming period of pansies, camellias, azaleas, and traditional spring flowering bulbs. Within recent years Charleston gardeners have discovered that with new and improved varieties of annuals and perennials, the joys of an early summer garden can be easily achieved. Stokesia, daylily, balloon flower, blue salvia, liatris, shasta daisy, and yarrow are but a few of the perennials that now are commonly used.

A large rectangular brick terrace and two handsome lattice pavilions fill the back portion of the garden, creating an ideal area for outdoor dining and entertaining. A small garden pool with water jets on either side adds life and movement to this attractive outdoor space. The garden is made to appear larger than its actual size through the clever use of trompe l'oeil, an ingenious technique perfected by the French in the seventeenth and eighteenth centuries to create illusions of space. In the Coker garden this technique is employed through the use of a cleverly placed arched mirror and trompe l'oeil latticework created by Charleston iron smith Rich Aurett.

Coker Garden Plan

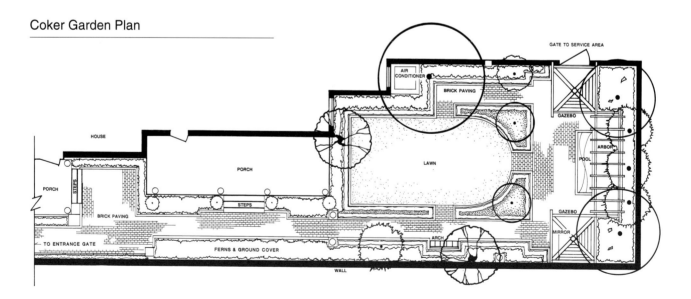

82

A colorful border of spring and summer blooming plants surrounds an oval stretch of lawn which serves as the centerpiece of the garden.

An arched mirror is used to create an illusion of space, making the garden appear larger than its actual size.

Garden of the Colonel William Rhett House

Originally owned by Colonel William Rhett, famous in the early history of Charleston for his capture of the dreaded pirate Stede Bonnet and his crew in 1719, the William Rhett House (ca. 1712) is one of the oldest structures in the city. Presently owned by Mr. and Mrs. Andrew Drury, the existing gardens are based on a design prepared in the 1940s by internationally known landscape architect Umberto Innocenti of Long Island, New York. At the time Innocenti prepared his design, the William Rhett House was owned by Mr. and Mrs. Benjamin Kittredge, who in 1927 created Charleston's famous Cypress Gardens which feature enormous cypress trees, reflecting water and brilliant azaleas in a beautiful natural setting along the Cooper River.

While each of the individual gardens comprising the William Rhett property have their own individual character and charm, the most dramatic is the parterre garden located on the west side of the house. Its simple well-proportioned beds, surrounded by a lovely brick and stucco wall, creates a striking view from the piazza above. Access to the garden is provided by a decorative wrought-iron gate painted a soft shade of blue. The central portion of the garden is paved in old Charleston brick and features a centrally located sundial. Small statues in each corner are replicas of the four seasons. Individual beds are bordered in Japanese box (*Buxus microphylla* var. *japonica*) and planted with azaleas to create a colorful springtime display. The simple beauty and elegance of this garden make it a pleasure to experience any season of the year. Included on the grounds are a majestic grove of live oak trees (*Quercus virginiana*) underplanted with Algerian ivy (*Hedera canariensis*), a formal terrace paved in antique brick, and several connecting gardens that are perfectly suited to their lovely eighteenth-century architectural setting.

A view from the piazza overlooking the formal parterre garden. Beds are edged with Japanese box and planted with azaleas for a striking springtime display.

The parterre garden contains a sundial, small stone statues, and several fanciful pieces of topiary in the shape of deer. Behind the ivy-covered wall lies a magnificent grove of live oak trees that form a lovely canopy of green.

A view of one of the many outdoor rooms that comprise the garden of the William Rhett House. A tree-form Carolina jessamine (*Gelsemium sempervirens*) is silhouetted against the stained glass window of a neighboring church.

The Garden of the Jonathan Badger House

Located on the lower end of Tradd Street in Charleston's historic district, the Jonathan Badger House is a pre-revolutionary brick double tenement believed to have been built around 1746. Beginning at the street and extending the full length of the property, the garden is divided into three distinct landscaped spaces, each affording different levels of privacy and accommodating special activities and needs.

Opening directly onto Tradd Street, the first and most public of the garden spaces serves as an arrival court that affords access to the main entrance of the house and also serves as an attractive off-street parking area. Paved in antique brick and bluestone, the entrance court is surrounded on two sides by a handsome brick wall and planting beds that not only soften the effects of the paving but also serve as a transition between the arrival court and the more private and secluded garden areas beyond. An heir-loom joggling board and potted plants provide interest and add to the visual character of the area.

The second and more secluded area of the garden is entered through a decorative wrought-iron gate that opens onto a spacious terrace overlooking an oval panel of grass surrounded on three sides by a planting of seasonal flowers, trees, and shrubs. This outdoor space includes such traditional favorites as camellias, azaleas, a chaste tree, crape myrtle, and a variety of spring and summer blooming plants.

The third and most private of the individual garden spaces provides a complete sense of seclusion. A large banana plant (*Musa paradisiaca*), ginger lilies (*Hedychium coronarium*), fatsia (*Fatsia japonica*), and other shade-loving plants help to create a lush subtropical oasis and afford the opportunity to attract birds to this quiet, peaceful sanctuary. A pair of garden buildings, an attractive vine-covered arbor, and a small wall fountain are perfect additions to this delightful garden retreat.

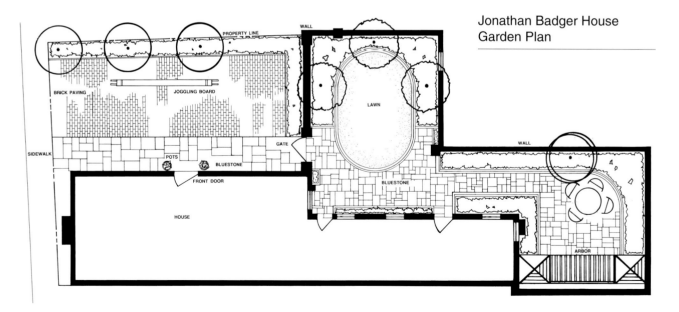

Jonathan Badger House
Garden Plan

86

A view of the most secluded of three outdoor rooms that comprise the Jonathan Badger House garden. This peaceful sanctuary is filled with a variety of shade-loving plants protected by high garden walls.

A Secret Garden

Inspired by Frances Hodgson Burnett's legendary book *The Secret Garden,* this small secluded garden is located in historic Ansonborough—an area that developed after 1746 as one of Charleston's first suburban neighborhoods. From the street there is little evidence of the tiny garden that is hidden behind the high wall that extends the entire length of the property along historic Anson Street.

Entrance into the garden is gained through a simple but attractive wooden gate that incorporates a decorative cast-iron grille that was a gift to the owner when the garden was first developed. Once inside the gate, the garden immediately unfolds revealing a delightful series of outdoor spaces each with its own individual character and charm. To the left of the entrance the eye is drawn to a formal area of the garden, paved in old Charleston brick and tastefully planted with Japanese box, Asian jasmine (*Trachelospermum asiaticum*), and cherry laurels (*Prunus caroliniana*). The cherry laurels have been allowed to grow into small trees creating a wonderful canopy of green and providing protection against the heat of the late afternoon sun. A beautiful eighteenth-century statue of the Little Shepherdess serves as a focal point of the planting and adds an appropriate sense of scale. To the right of the entrance is a small service area cleverly concealed behind a decorative wrought-iron fence and gate.

Above, a small formal area to the left of the entrance gate is planted with Japanese box, Asian jasmine, and cherry laurel to create a green garden that can be enjoyed year-round.

Below is a view from the house to the entrance gate. A large tree-form ligustrum provides refreshing shade in summer, and its sculptured branches add interest and character to the garden in winter.

A formal walk extends from the entrance gate along a central axis to an attractive flagstone terrace which serves as the centerpiece of the garden. This delightful sitting area is shaded by a beautiful tree-form ligustrum (*Ligustrum japonicum*) planted underneath with Asian jasmine—a low-growing evergreen vine. A small fluted birdbath provides a perfect accent to the design and attracts many birds to the garden—especially in early morning and late afternoon.

The walk continues to a raised brick terrace which is furnished with an antique love seat and two comfortable chairs that encourage one to relax and enjoy the beauty of this tranquil retreat. Two large pots planted with evergreen Japanese viburnum (*Viburnum japonicum*) are located on opposite ends of the terrace to provide balance and scale.

One of the most fascinating features of the garden is the extensive use of accessories collected by the owner over the last forty years. Elegant French fire-irons, decorative Mexican pots and sculpture, and several small bronze statues are selectively placed throughout the garden to create visual interest and to add a touch of personal charm. Because of the garden's limited space, pots of flowering plants are added for color and seasonal interest—geraniums in spring, impatiens (*Impatiens wallerana*) in summer, and poinsettias (*Euphorbia pulcherrima*) in winter. This delightful city garden represents the collective talents of many friends and associates of the owner who offered ideas, advice, and inspiration to create a garden that reflects a true labor of love.

A view from the gate along the central axis of the garden showing the small flagstone terrace and tasteful use of garden accessories.

An existing garage was cleverly transformed into an attractive garden structure complete with flagstone terrace and vine-covered arbor.

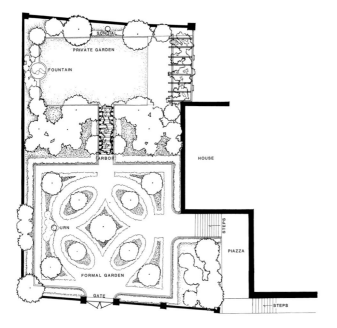

Hanahan Garden Plan

Hanahan Garden

Located on South Battery in Charleston's historic district, the Hanahan garden contains two distinct outdoor rooms—a re-created parterre garden and an informal private garden designed for contemporary needs. When Charleston landscape architects Hugh and Mary Palmer Dargan were commissioned to design the Hanahan garden, little did they know that they would uncover remnants of an earlier garden of late eighteenth- or early nineteenth-century design. Following extensive research, it was determined that the layout of the original garden was in fact similar to other small patterned gardens that were common in Charleston during earlier times. This in turn prompted the decision to preserve the existing garden layout and to restore the garden to its original design. Through the sensitive use of old garden ornaments, authentic details, and heirloom plants, this restored garden serves as an outstanding example of period design. Antique plants selected for the garden to create a sense of age and to present the garden within an appropriate historical context include old garden favorites such as violas, tulips, camellias, Indian azaleas (*Azalea indica*), tea roses, crape myrtle (*Lagerstroemia indica*), and trumpet vine (*Campsis radicans*).

While the front garden conforms to a distinct period design, the adjoining private garden located at the rear of the property is based on a complementary twentieth-century plan. This contemporary garden includes a spacious blue-stone terrace, a wisteria-covered arbor, a small fountain, and a perfectly proportioned stretch of lawn that provides ample space for entertaining and a variety of social activities. Even though the two gardens are different in function they are skillfully combined into a totally integrated and unified design.

A view of the parterre garden from the piazza reveals a pattern comprised of four ovals surrounded by a central diamond with concave sides. Bricks are used to edge the formal beds and to define the garden paths.

A rose-covered arbor serves as a transition between the formal parterre and the adjoining private garden which is more contemporary in design.

Colorful window boxes and lush plantings of maidenhair ferns entice visitors along a small narrow lane to an attractive garden gate.

A Garden Designed for Entertaining

The garden of Patti and Joseph (Peter) McGee is a delightful series of garden rooms joined by two brick archways creating a masterpiece of spatial design. Located near Charleston's historic Dock Street Theater on the upper end of Church Street, access to the McGees' garden is by way of a long narrow lane that leads to a small entry gate. Visitors are enticed along the lane and into the garden by a sequence of colorful window boxes filled with seasonal plants—pansies, alyssum, dusty miller, geraniums, and verbena. The lane is paved in an oval pattern of old Charleston brick and is flanked along both sides by a lush planting of southern maidenhair ferns (*Adiantum capillus-veneris*).

Once inside the gate the garden continues along a brick-paved walk which expands into two walled courtyards. From a spacious sunroom located at the back of the house, french doors open onto the garden creating an uninterrupted arrangement of free-flowing space. The McGees redesigned their garden in 1986 to achieve a more functional plan that provided good circulation and could be used for small and informal receptions associated with Spoleto—Charleston's international festival of classical arts.

With the assistance of landscape architects Hugh and Mary Palmer Dargan, several basic changes were made in the garden's original design. One of the problems associated with the garden was that circulation between the two courtyards was obstructed by a small storage house that separated the garden into two independent rooms. By reducing the storage structure, or little house as it was called, to two-thirds of its original size, an additional entry could be added between the two garden rooms, thus opening what

Sheltered by high walls, this small garden room is used for outdoor receptions and entertaining. Its charm is created by lush evergreen plants and a tasteful assortment of colorful pots, decorative furnishings, and attractive garden accessories.

A decorative wood arbor helps unify the two garden rooms and provides the benefit of shade during summer.

garden and using it as a means of further unifying the two garden rooms.

The garden is filled with an array of flowering and evergreen plants that make it a constant source of enjoyment and pleasure throughout the year. The surrounding high walls are covered with evergreen clematis (*Clematis armandi*), star jasmine (*Trachelospermum jasminoides*), creeping fig (*Ficus pumila*), and cat's claw vine (*Macfadyena unguis-cati*). These evergreen vines not only soften the garden walls but also provide fragrance and color throughout spring and early summer. Shady parts of the garden are planted with fatsia (*Fatsia japonica*), variegated aucuba (*Aucuba japonica variegata*), and Japanese yew (*Podocarpus macrophyllus*). Camellias and azaleas provide color in spring along with a peppermint peach and flowering crabapple. A large loquat (*Eriobotrya japonica*) and camphor tree (*Cinnamomum camphora*) create a canopy of green and help cool the garden during the hot summer months. Being an ardent gardener and connoisseur of plants, Patti enjoys growing a variety of unusual and interesting plants. Many of these are planted in pots and decorative containers which are placed throughout the garden to create many colorful and artistic compositions.

As in other Charleston gardens, careful attention has been given to the selection and use of many garden features to add charm and character to the garden. Small wall sculptures are strategically located on the high brick walls amid the tracery of evergreen vines. Antique wrought-iron furniture adds a decorative note and affords an opportunity to sit and savor the joys of the garden. A small walled fountain serves as a focal point and the sound of water adds an additional dimension to the many moods of this delightful Charleston garden.

had originally been an isolated space. Old Charleston bricks salvaged from the little house were used to create arched doorways into the second courtyard and for additional paving which helped to unify the overall design.

An additional problem that had to be solved was that the little house supported a magnificent Lady Banksia rose that was the focal point of the garden each spring. To solve this problem, the Dargans designed an attractive arbor on which the rose could be trained, thus retaining it as an integral part of the

A magnificent Lady Banksia rose serves as the central focal
point of the garden in spring.

Plan of the Heyward Washington House Garden

Heyward-Washington House Garden

The Heyward-Washington House is one of the most historic houses in America—once the home of Thomas Heyward, a signer of the Declaration of Independence, and the temporary residence of President George Washington when he visited Charleston in 1791. Also important in Charleston's historic preservation movement, the Heyward-Washington House is the first dwelling to have been restored and operated as a house museum.

When the house was purchased by the Charleston Museum in 1929, no vestige of a garden remained: only concrete, bricks, and several miscellaneous outbuildings. In an effort to create a period garden that would complement the house and grounds, the late Emma Richardson, assistant director of the Charleston Museum, was given the task of creating a garden that would exemplify a late eighteenth-century Charleston garden design.

After consulting many old garden plans, including the layout of the Miles Brewton House garden (ca. 1769), Richardson developed an attractive geometric design consisting of a long rectangle incorporating a circular motif with concentric paths and brick-bordered beds. The work of laying out the garden was performed by Richardson with the help of an assistant and the use of a yardstick and piece of string. While efforts to implement the garden plan were initiated in the 1930s, the final layout remained unfinished until 1941.

Since George Washington had resided in the Heyward-Washington House in 1791, it was decided that only plants introduced into cultivation prior to that date should be used. Many friends gave old-fashioned plants from their gardens while others gave small monetary gifts. Some of the plants

96

received by Richardson for use in the garden included Cherokee roses, crape myrtle, jessamine (*Gelsemium sempervirens*), alyssum, iris, lantana (*Lantana camara*), snowdrops, narcissi bulbs, japonicas, woodbine (*Lonicera sempervirens*), orange trees, gardenias (*Gardenia jasminoides*), and box.

Refinements in the planting and design of the garden took place in 1965 with the assistance of the Garden Club of Charleston and the professional advice of landscape architect Loutrel Briggs. Included in these efforts were the selection and placement of additional heirloom plants and the creation of a small herb garden developed in an intricate design. The charming character of this lovely old garden is achieved through its well-proportioned design, collection of heirloom plants, and wonderful sense of age.

A view of the Heyward Washington House garden in late spring. The garden contains a central feature encircled with a colorful planting of stock, dianthus, pansies, and phlox.

The use of heirloom plants adds to the historic character and charm of the Heyward Washington House garden. A planting of *Gladious byzantinus,* native to the eastern Mediterranean region, adds a splash of color to the garden in early summer.

Garden Features

There is no one who does not enjoy the first walk through a garden that he has not previously seen. There is perhaps first the pleasure of the disposition of space, whether open or enclosed, architectural or green. Then follows the appreciation of detail.

G. A. Jellicoe, *The Book of Garden Ornament*

Garden features and details such as gates, walls, fences, benches, pools, and sculptures play an important role in providing the finishing touches to a garden. They allow for individual expression and the opportunity to reflect the interest and personality of the owner. Garden features and details are particularly useful in the small garden for it is here they receive special attention and help to establish a garden's overall image and mood. Because of limited space and the greater perception of detail in the small garden, special care must be given to garden features to achieve the most dramatic results. It is the creative use of garden features and a genius for details that give Charleston's small gardens their special character and visual appeal.

Walls

Old garden walls are one of the most prominent and treasured of garden features. They not only provide enclosure and protection but also create a wonderful sense of privacy which can exclude the outside world. Garden walls are also useful in defining spatial boundaries, screening views, and creating permanent outdoor rooms. Many Charleston gardens are surrounded by walls 7 or 8 feet high and, as noted by Shaffer in *Carolina Gardens*, the garden walls of Charleston are one of the most important and distinctive features of the city:

First are the high brick walls of which strangers sometimes complain but later learn to love; for to the passer-by there is here the fascination of enticing glimpses, the lure and mystery of half revealed Edens; to the garden guest the blessed sense of seclusion, the rare charm of being alone with beauty, the world shut out. . . . The Walls are of brick of English origin or measure and are laid in English bond. They often curve upward to meet the house wall, so making house and garden a closer unit. A lovely detail occurs in the "blind arches" that sometimes face the garden side—the extrusive arches of brick, the recessed intervening surfaces faced with pink or buff plaster or weathered tabby.

Many walls in Charleston contain decorative wrought iron gates or clairvoyées, which permit limited views and glimpses of the gardens that lie within.

Another important feature of Charleston's high garden walls are the benefits they afford in protection from the harsh effects of sun and wind during summer, and the added warmth they provide during the winter when the heat of the sun is stored by the walls during the day and gradually released at night. Within these sheltered environments, or microclimates, grow a multitude of exotic and tender plants that give Charleston's gardens their subtropical feeling.

The ideal way to see Charleston is to stroll about the streets peering over ancient walls and wrought-iron gates into small gardens and courtyards, discovering the hundreds of fascinating details that reflect the city's treasured past.

Fences

Fences, while less formidable than garden walls, are also useful in creating privacy and enclosure. One of the greatest advantages of a picket fence over a garden wall is good ventilation which helps to cool the garden during hot summer days. Like the beautiful picket fences of New England's villages and towns, Charleston can also boast of many fine examples which vary from simple to elaborate designs. Fences are particularly useful in Charleston because of the city's many narrow lots and dense urban form.

Many of Charleston's picket fences were designed by the same artisans who built the fashionable and elegant houses they surround. Great care was taken by early builders in the design and construction of fences. They were considered an integral part of the entire design and, as such, reflect the materials and details of the house and its ornamentation. Landscape paintings of nineteenth-century Lowcountry scenes by Charleston artist Charles Fraser (1782–1800) provide visual documentation of many wooden fences that surrounded and subdivided city and county seats. Charleston's picket fences generally express a simple rhythm and harmony of solids and voids and contain turned, square, or flat pickets which were traditionally painted white or Charleston green.

A handsome wall with arches provides a perfect backdrop for Charleston's historic Washington Park.

Gates

By tradition a gate serves as a doorway or entrance into a garden and, as such, plays an important role in establishing the mood and character of the garden within. Both the design and height of a gate are important considerations in determining the image of the garden and the level of privacy desired.

In order to create a unified and appropriate design, it is essential that a garden gate reflect and harmonize with the architectural character of the house and its surroundings.

Gates have been an important architectural feature in Charleston since colonial times, providing access from the street into the city's enclosed gardens and service yards. Charleston's early wrought-iron gates reflected English patterns and designs and were often painted hues of blue or green with accents of gold—a sharp contrast to the black ironwork generally found in Charleston today. Many of Charleston's finest gates were fashioned during the antebellum period by well-known German ironworkers, including Christopher Werner—best known for the design of the beautiful sword gates on Legare Street. By the mid-nineteenth-century wrought iron was replaced by cast iron, which was increasingly used to fashion gates, fences, statues, fountains, urns, benches, and lamps.

While Charleston's gates create a sense of security for those within and of exclusion for those without, their open designs provide the opportunity for visual enjoyment and glimpses of small gardens that are hidden behind protective walls. These limited but enticing views of Charleston's gardens are considered one of the city's greatest delights.

Surface Materials

Of all the physical elements that enter into a garden's design, surface materials are by far the most important. They not only articulate movement but also define outdoor spaces and determine how a garden is used. Their proportion, texture, and scale are fundamental to the structure and character of a garden's overall design. Brick, flagstone, gravel,

Picket fences, often 4 to 5 feet tall, surround many Charleston gardens creating a sense of privacy and enclosure.

Decorative wrought-iron gates offer enticing views into many Charleston gardens, adding charm and character to the city.

cobblestone, or grass are all potential materials that can be used in creating an infinite array of patterns and designs. Materials should be selected on the basis of both aesthetic and practical concerns, taking into account durability, maintenance, and visual appeal as well as the character and style of the garden. The smaller the space the more attention surface materials should receive as they often become the focal point of the garden.

Traditional paving materials often found in Charleston's old gardens include Portland stone, Welch slate, Belgian blocks, cobblestone, and Bermuda limestone. These ancient and handsome materials were brought to the city in the ballast of sailing ships and over time found their way into many of Charleston's gardens and grounds. These in turn were supplemented with local materials including sandshell, crushed oyster shells, and old Charleston bricks for paths, walks, and drives. Old Charleston bricks were made at outlying plantations then carried down the Ashley and Cooper rivers for use in the city. Color variations characteristic of many of these antique bricks are generally attributed to uneven temperatures in the rustic kilns or from sand that was left accidently on the unbaked clay.

By tradition, if a gate is left open in spring when gardens are at their peak of bloom, it serves as an invitation to step inside and enjoy the garden within.

Cobblestone, old brick, and flagstone are cleverly combined into many interesting patterns and designs.

A decorative paving pattern enhances an entrance court on Bedon's Alley.

Water

Of the many features that can be used in a small garden, water offers the greatest opportunity of all. Appropriately described as the living spirit or soul of a garden, water has the ability to focus attention on itself as few other garden features can. Any opportunity to use water in a garden should always be taken, for a garden always seems to fall short of its full potential when water is missing.

Water can create many moods, ranging from the quiet serenity of a tranquil pool to the animated movement of a splashing fountain. The sound and movement of water appeal to the senses and add relief and coolness to a garden on a hot summer day. Another advantage of water is its ability to reflect surrounding surfaces and to add a sense of light, depth, and spaciousness to the smallest space. The reflecting surface of a small garden pool is in effect comparable to the use of a mirror in an indoor room. It reflects colors of flowers and the green of shrubs and trees. Water can be employed in many ways ranging from a simple pool to lure the eye and create illusion to a small wall fountain to add life and movement. Water features including ornamental lakes, canals, pools, ponds, and sheets of water were frequently mentioned in accounts of old Charleston gardens. As early as 1764 the *South Carolina Gazette* advertised the services of John Barnes, a garden-architect, to assist Charleston gardeners in erecting water works, such as fountains, cascades, grottos.

A decorative wall fountain adds the alluring sound of water to a Legare Street garden.

Seats and Benches

A comfortable and attractive seat or bench where one can sit and enjoy the garden is one of life's greatest pleasures. In addition to providing a comfortable and convenient place to rest and relax, seats and benches can also serve as a garden feature or focal point. The location, material, and style of outdoor furniture are as important to a garden as interior furnishings are to an indoor room. Whether seats or benches are made of stone, wood, or metal depends to a great degree on the design of the garden and surrounding materials.

Charleston is well known for its contribution to garden furniture through the development of the Charleston bench, sometimes referred to as the Battery bench. This decorative and durable structure is made of wooden slats set between ornamental cast-iron ends. Originally designed as a park bench or settee around 1880, the Charleston bench was first used along the Battery and in White Point Garden in an effort to improve the city's parks and pleasure grounds. With its delicate design and beautiful ornamental details, the Charleston bench soon made its way into many city gardens where it is found today as a traditional garden feature.

A Victorian wrought-iron bench (top) provides a welcome place to relax in a small State Street garden while a traditional Battery bench adds charm to Charleston's historic Rainbow Row (bottom).

Sculpture

Sculpture has been described as an expression of the creative spirit of man and has been used in gardens in some form or another since Roman times. A piece of sculpture of the right size and shape that is suitably placed can add tremendous interest and visual appeal to the smallest of gardens. For best results sculpture must relate to the scale of the garden and be displayed against an appropriate background, whether it is a wall, fence, or a natural setting of foliage. While sculpture should always harmonize with its surroundings, its placement is usually more important than the material of which it is made—stone, metal, or wood. Sculpture may be representational or abstract in design depending on personal taste and how it is to be used. To be truly successful, sculpture should always appear to be an integral part of a garden's overall design.

Traditional sculpture is employed as the central focal element in a Tradd Street garden.

Garden Structures

Garden structures—including gazebos, pergolas, pavilions, arbors, and summerhouses—have always been popular garden features and are as much at home in the small garden as in one of considerable size. The uses of garden structures range from providing protection against sun, wind, or rain to creating a sheltered retreat which invites relaxation and repose. Traditionally located at the intersection of paths or at the end of an axis, garden structures can serve as a focal point or as a feature to complement an architectural theme.

Garden structures are particularly useful in Southern gardens where they provide protection from the hot summer sun. Their use in Charleston was noted as early as 1718 by a Swiss traveler to the city: "the Inconveniency from the Heat during that Time (June, July and August) is made easier by shady Groves, open airy Rooms, Arbors and Summer-houses" (in Lockwood, vol. 2). Frequently covered with climbing roses or ornamental vines, these decorative garden features were usually of light and delicate designs. Construction generally consisted of interlaced lattice over a solid frame or, more traditionally, involved a combination of wood panels, solid roof, and lattice design. Garden structures were as a rule square, rectangular, or octagonal in form and varied from simple to fanciful designs.

A barrel-vaulted arbor is covered in spring with the riotous blooms of a magnificent Lady Banksia rose and *Rosa chinensis mutablis*, the butterfly rose.

Containers

Pots, tubs, and urns make a delightful addition to any garden, large or small. They can be used as decorative elements on their own or can be planted with flowers, bulbs, or vines to provide a splash of color through the spring, summer, and fall seasons. Containers can be obtained in a variety of shapes, sizes, and materials to meet the needs of any garden regardless of size or design. The selected container should be carefully considered to ensure that it is appropriate to the character and style of the garden.

Particularly useful in the small garden where planting area is limited, containers help maximize the use of available space and can be moved about to create an endless array of seasonal delights. Special care and consideration must be given to the selection and maintenance of plants grown in containers to insure that they always look their best and enhance the garden setting.

A variety of sun- and shade-loving plants lend themselves to container gardening with geraniums, impatiens, Madagascar periwinkle, petunias, and begonias being some of the most versatile and satisfactory. An endless array of plant compositions combining shapes, colors, and textures can be developed for use on patios, terraces, balconies, and stairs.

Containers offer a wonderful opportunity to create an endless array of colorful plant compositions for use on patios, terraces, balconies, stairs, and entrances.

Window Boxes

Window boxes afford a wonderful opportunity to enhance the look and appearance of a house and can be enjoyed equally from both indoors and outdoors. Long a favorite in Europe and the Mediterranean region, window boxes have gained increased popularity in America because of limited time and space for gardening and the endless opportunities

Window boxes are especially useful in Charleston where
many of the city's eighteenth- and nineteenth-century houses
were built directly on the street, affording little space for
gardening in the traditional manner.

they provide for creating colorful and imaginative floral displays.

Ready made window boxes of wood or metal are available in many shapes and sizes or can easily be built to suit specific needs and desires. Whatever the selection or size, it is essential that a window box be strong enough to hold the weight of water-soaked soil and be securely attached to the house or window ledge with metal rackets that are both durable and strong.

The planting possibilities for window boxes are limited only by one's imagination. They can be changed several times a season or even on a weekly basis, employing a combination of bulbs, annuals, perennials, herbs, and miniature shrubs. Window boxes are particularly useful in Charleston where many of the city's eighteenth- and nineteenth-century houses were built directly on the street, affording little space for gardening in the traditional manner. They are also useful on windows facing onto the city's narrow garden lanes, where they provide enticing displays of seasonal color along pathways leading to secluded gardens tucked away at the rear of houses. Plants frequently grown in Charleston's window boxes include pansies, English daisies, alyssum, calendulas, snapdragons, and flowering bulbs in spring, followed by petunias, ageratum, lobelia, begonias, geraniums, and impatiens in summer and fall.

Ornaments and Accessories

Ornaments and accessories have tremendous potential for use in the garden when proper thought is given to their selection and placement. They can provide pleasure and delight and draw attention to a particular area of the garden. Like other garden features, they should relate to the setting and fit into the overall scheme. Ornaments and accessories add character and personality and can be enjoyed throughout the year. In a small garden they should be used with restraint, otherwise the garden will take on a confused and cluttered appearance. The range and choice of ornaments and accessories are almost endless and include such items as sundials, spheres, vases, urns, birdbaths, terra-cotta pots, finials, columns, and tiles. The joggling board is an unusual garden accessory often found in Charleston gardens. Originally built in the early 1800s as an exercise device, it soon became popular for recreation, relaxation, and even courting. Today the joggling board frequently can be found on piazzas and in gardens throughout the city where it has become a Charleston tradition.

Often found in gardens or on piazzas, the joggling board has become a cherished Charleston tradition.

111

Plants of Charleston Gardens

One of the most interesting and fascinating aspects of Charleston gardens centers around the vast array of plants associated with the city's gardening tradition. Over the years a distinctive palette of Charleston garden plants has evolved, comprising many native species as well as imported ornamentals from Europe, the West Indies, South America, Africa, and Asia. This unusual and unique collection of indigenous and imported plants has developed for several different reasons: Charleston's position as a major seaport city, a wealth of native plants found in the area, the influence of early botanists and gardeners, and Charleston's favorable climate.

Charleston's early development as a major seaport tied it to the vast trade routes that connected England and other European ports by way of the Azores and the West Indies. From these connections came traditional plants from Europe as well as a wide variety of exotic seeds, bulbs, fruits, and flowering plants from remote corners of the world. In addition to plants from European nations such as England, Holland, and France, many tropical and subtropical plants arrived from the West Indies. These plants came to Charleston by way of early settlers from the English West Indies, particularly Barbados, who brought with them plants native to the Caribbean Islands and South America. Included were the yellow bignonia or cat's claw vine (*Macfadyena unguiscati*), a tenacious vine covering many Charleston walls and buildings; lantana (*Lantana camara*) and four-o'clock (*Mirabilis jalapa*), both flowering perennials commonly grown in old Charleston gardens; Jerusalem thorn (*Parkinsonia aculeata*), a small, flowering tree with prolific yellow flowers grown for its unusual aesthetic appeal; and acacia (*Acacia farnesiana*), a small tree or shrub prized for its highly fragrant flowers used in making perfume.

The lush coastal forest of the Carolina Lowcountry contained many native trees, flowers, and vines immediately identified by the early settlers for their ornamental value. According to Shaffer in *Carolina Gardens*, "the first Europeans who reached the shores of what is South Carolina were astonished by the natural beauty of the scene, for here nature had so prepared the stage, through waiting ages, that verdant strand and flower-decked river shore appeared to the sea weary voyagers as the fabled Garden of Hesperides." From this wealth of native flora many plants of the region soon found their way into Charleston. Even today Charleston gardeners rely on many of these indigenous plants to embellish and enhance their gardens. Trumpet vine (*Campsis radicans*) festoons many a Charleston wall pro-

Charleston—The Celebrated Southern Port Over the Rooftops in 1870 by John Stobart

With one of the largest and most beautiful landlocked harbors in the world, Charleston soon developed into a major seaport. From Europe came traditional seeds, bulbs, and plants in exchange for a fascinating array of native flora that flourished in the Carolina Lowcountry.

viding orange trumpet-shaped flowers from May to October, Carolina jessamine (*Gelsemium sempervirens*) produces a profusion of showy fragrant yellow flowers in early spring, sweetbay magnolia (*Magnolia virginiana*) is grown for its evergreen foliage and sweetly scented flowers, and the stately palmetto (*Sabal palmetto*) lines many

Charleston streets and boulevards.

Native plants were also collected from the wild and sent to Europe as newfound treasures. Carolina jessamine (*Gelsemium sempervirens*) was introduced into England from Virginia as early as 1640, Carolina allspice (*Calycanthus floridus*) made its way to England by 1726, and the southern magnolia (*Mag-*

113

nolia grandiflora) was sent from Carolina in 1734. As an indication of the flourishing interest in plants from the New World, the *South Carolina Gazette,* Charleston's first newspaper, reported that from 31 October 1766 to 8 May 1767 five casks of seeds and forty boxes of trees, shrubs, and plants of various kinds were shipped from the port of Charleston.

Another important factor contributing to Charleston's rich plant heritage centers around the work of early botanists and gardeners. Significant among these are Dr. Alexander Garden, Henry Laurens, John Watson, Martha Logan, André Michaux, and Thomas Walter. Each played an important role either by introducing native plants into cultivation or enriching Charleston's gardens with a variety of new plants from abroad. The gardenia (*Gardenia jasminoides*), tea olive (*Osmanthus fragrans*), crape myrtle (*Lagerstroemia indica*), loblolly bay (*Gordonia lasianthus*), Carolina allspice (*Calycanthus floridus*), fringe tree (*Chionanthus virginicus*), and the mimosa (*Albizia julibrissin*) are but a few of the many native and imported plants introduced into Charleston by early botanists and gardeners. Advertisements in early newspapers provide a valuable record of local offerings of seed, bulbs, and ornamentals. One of the earliest of these was in 1731 in the *South Carolina Gazette* by Samuel Eveleigh advertising "divers sorts of best garden seeds." This was soon followed by similar advertisements from other seed merchants and nursery owners offering Charleston gardeners a vast array of fruit trees, flower roots, seeds, bulbs, and choice ornamentals. Charleston gardeners still rely on many of these early introductions and selections to create the wonderful array of seasonal plants that make the city's gardens so appealing.

Charleston's favorable climate, long growing season, and sheltered gardens enclosed by high walls afford a unique opportunity to grow many tender and subtropical plants similar to those found in more temperate regions of the world. An account of a visit to Charleston by Lieutenant Francis Hall in 1819 provides this observation: "On entering the City, we seemed to be transported into a garden. Orange trees laden with ripe oranges, peach trees covered with blossoms, and flowering shrubs which I had been accustomed to see only in hot houses, gave me the impression similar to those which I suppose you experience on visiting some of the cities on the Mediterranean." Charleston's climate does approximate conditions found in certain parts of the Mediterranean region. Many plants typically associated with that area of the world such as the oleander (*Nerium oleander*), fig (*Ficus carica*), calendula (*Calendula officinalis*), and snapdragon (*Antirrhnum majus*) can be found in Charleston gardens today.

Oranges were frequently grown in Charleston during the eighteenth century and were often listed among the products of the colony. An advertisement in the *South Carolina Gazette* in 1737 notes that James Kerr of Charleston offered for sale "a large quantity of oranges, all picked by hand and as good as when taken from the tree." In 1745 orange, lemon, and lime trees could be purchased from Richard Lake at his plantation on the Ashley River. Spacious groves of both Sweet and Seville oranges were found in Charleston before the Revolution along what is presently Orange Street and in the vicinity of the Powder Magazine on Cumberland Street. A visitor to the city in the early 1800s (quoted in Lockwood) observed that oranges were also grown in many Charleston gardens: "the houses of the suburbs were, for the most part, surrounded by gardens, in which orange

Ruby-throated Humming Bird.
TROCHILUS COLUBRIS.

Trumpet Vine (*Campsis radicans*) from Audubon's *The Birds of America*

A native plant found in Southern fields and forests, the trumpet vine is often grown in Charleston gardens where its bright orange, tubular-shaped flowers occur in great profusion from early summer to late fall. Illustration courtesy of the Charleston Museum, Charleston, South Carolina.

Oranges were grown in great abundance in Charleston during the eighteenth century and were frequently listed as exports of the colony.

trees, with most splendid ripe fruit, monthly roses in full bloom, and a variety of other flourishing plants displayed themselves." Over time the growing of oranges in Charleston began to decline as noted in J. T. L. Shecut's *Medical and Philosophical Essays of 1819:* "The Rev. Mr. Hewitt, has recorded a frost which happened on the 7th of February, 1747, remarkable for its severity, destroying most of the orange trees, in and near the town. . . . Oranges, through plentiful forty or fifty years ago, are now raised with difficulty. This is certainly . . . proof of the change of our climate." Whether due to a colder climate or simply because oranges became easier to obtain from other sources, the growing of the fruit in Charleston had greatly diminished by the middle of the nineteenth century.

A unique combination of natural, physical, and historical factors has been responsible for creating the rich diversity of plants found in Charleston gardens today. A representative list of traditional Charleston garden plants has been compiled that includes information on plant origin, physical characteristics, landscape use, and general growing conditions. While in no way inclusive, this list does provide a description of plants frequently used and grown in Charleston gardens today. Although many of these plants were grown in the city's historic gardens, they are still both appealing and appropriate for contemporary use.

TRADITIONAL PLANTS GROWN IN CHARLESTON GARDENS

Vines, Ground Covers, Shrubs, and Trees

Althaea (*Hibiscus syriacus*)

Native to China and India, althaea, or Rose of Sharon, as it is frequently called, is a deciduous shrub or small tree introduced to America before 1790. Planted by Thomas Jefferson at Monticello and mentioned by George Washington in his diary, althaea has survived over the years as a common garden shrub because of its hardy nature and ability to adapt to a variety of growing conditions.

Reaching a height of 10 to 15 feet, althaea develops a slender, upright form that becomes more rounded and spreading with age. Medium-textured, dark green foliage is produced with little or no fall color. This plant's main attraction is its hollyhock-like flowers that bloom continuously from June until frost. Flowers can be single or double, ranging in color from pure white to pink and bluish-purple to rose. Brown seed pods of little ornamental value are produced in late fall and winter.

Often used as an attractive specimen or as an addition to a shrub border, althaea also makes a good hedge. It is an ideal plant where quick growth, extended color, and low maintenance are desired. Grown in both sun and partial shade, althaea tolerates a variety of soils and is resistant to most pest and diseases. Light pruning encourages additional blooms. Many new single and double cultivars are available in a variety of colors.

Aspidistra (*Aspidistra elatior*)

A native of China, aspidistra is a coarse-textured, herbaceous perennial that is widely grown through-out the South particularly in shady gardens. Commonly referred to as "cast-iron plant" because of its ability to tolerate low light and dry conditions, it is an excellent choice for difficult garden spaces or for locations offering less than ideal growing conditions.

The large, dark green leafy foliage of aspidistra is quite showy and adds an interesting sculptured effect to the landscape. Growing to an ultimate height of 2 feet, the lush, dark green leaves of aspidistra rise directly from the ground, forming large, upright leafy clumps that spread by means of underground stems.

Often used as a ground cover or as an accent plant because of its bold, exotic foliage, aspidistra can also be grown in pots or containers and used around patios and terraces for dramatic effect. With its slow rate of growth, it is excellent for small gardens with limited space.

Aspidistra benefits from a fertile and well-drained soil, low light, and protection from cold winter winds. A courtyard or a location under overhanging eaves is ideal for growing aspidistra. Pruning may be necessary to remove old, ragged, or damaged leaves, and to encourage fresh new foliage.

Banana Shrub (*Michelia figo*)

Native to China, banana shrub receives its name from the pleasant banana-like fragrance produced by small, magnolia-like flowers. A longtime favorite of southern gardeners and an excellent, large evergreen shrub for residential use, it is no longer grown as frequently as it was in the past.

Growing to a height of 10 to 15 feet, banana shrub develops into an upright, oval form rich and refined in character. Leaves are glossy, dark green, and elliptical in shape and grow to be approximately 3 inches long. Its compact habit of growth gives the appearance of a shrub that has been lightly pruned. Small creamy yellow flowers, edged in maroon, are produced in midspring. These produce a banana scented fragrance prominent on warm days and in the early afternoon.

Often used as a foundation plant or as a garden specimen, banana shrub also can be shaped easily into a small tree by removing the lower branches. Growing both in sun or partial shade, it prefers a moist, fertile, slightly acidic soil and good drainage. Long lived and slow growing, banana shrub is free from pests and plant diseases and requires little or no pruning.

Camellia (*Camellia japonica*)

Native to China and Japan, the camellia is reported to have been introduced into Charleston by

French botanist André Michaux before the end of the eighteenth century. In 1818 David Landreth, a Philadelphia seed merchant and one of the earliest growers of camellias in the country, opened a Charleston office which played a major role in the dissemination of camellias throughout the South up until the Civil War. Prized for its waxy, brightly colored flowers and beautiful evergreen foliage, the camellia is a popular ornamental shrub that has become a garden tradition in Southern gardens.

Blooming from late fall to early spring in colors ranging from pure white to deep red, with wide variations in between, the flowers of the camellia can be single, semi-double, or double in form. Camellias grow best in partial shade as understory plants where they benefit from filtered light and protection from hot midday sun.

An upright shrub with a somewhat oval form, the camellia is ideal for use in small gardens or foundation plantings and in pots and containers around patios and terraces. Old plants can be trained into small trees by careful pruning to expose lower limbs.

Camellias need rich, well-drained soil that is slightly acid. While numerous varieties of the camellia are available, several traditional varieties grown in Southern gardens include: *Pink Perfection* (light pink), *Professor Sargent* (brilliant red), *Daikagura* (rose and white), and *White Empress* (white).

Carolina Jessamine (*Gelsemium sempervirens*)

A native southeastern vine found growing from Virginia to Texas, Carolina jessamine has the distinction of being the state flower of South Carolina. Admired since colonial times as an ornamental, it was first sent to England around 1640. Carolina jessamine is one of the first native plants to bloom in spring, producing a profusion of showy, fragrant,

trumpet-shaped flowers in March and early April. Its waxy, evergreen leaves grow from 2 to 4 inches and often take on a reddish color in winter if grown in exposed locations. Because the twining stems of this evergreen vine are safe to use on wooden sur-

faces, it is highly recommended for arbors, pergolas, trellises, and fences. The cascading growth habit and fine-textured foliage of Carolina jessamine make it ideal for softening walls and garden structures.

Growing both in sun and shade, this versatile

119

and highly decorative vine is easy to grow and is free from insects and plant diseases. Because of its moderate growth, Carolina jessamine is one of the choicest vines for small gardens. While generally classified as a vine, Carolina jessamine also can be used effectively as a ground cover.

Cat's Claw Vine (*Macfadyena unguis-cati*)

Cat's claw vine is a native of an area extending from the West Indies to Argentina. It is commonly referred to by its earlier botanical names *Bignonia tweediana* and *Doxantha unguis-cati*. Often found growing on walls and buildings throughout Charleston and other southern coastal cities, its large, fleshy roots enable it to tolerate hot, dry conditions that few other plants can survive.

An evergreen climber, cat's claw vine has glossy, dark green foliage that adheres to almost any surface by means of tiny, tenacious, three-clawed tendrils from which it gets its name. In the spring it produces dense clusters of bright yellow, trumpet-shaped flowers which, unfortunately, are of short duration. An excellent vine for high walls or large surfaces needing screening, it benefits from annual pruning. This contains its growth, encourages new branches at its base, and eliminates the formation of unattractive seed pods which form during summer. Cat's claw vine prefers a sunny location and will grow in almost any

soil. It is relatively free of most plant diseases and insects and will tolerate cold to zero degrees.

While this vine has its limitations, its hardy nature and vigorous habit of growth make it a sound choice in difficult locations with adverse growing conditions.

Chaste Tree (*Vitex agnus-castus*)

Native to southern Europe and western Asia, chaste tree or spikenard as it is generally referred to

in Charleston, is a highly desirable, deciduous shrub long associated with old gardens. Chaste tree was mentioned by Thomas Jefferson in his *Garden Book* and by John Clayton, an English naturalist, in *Flora Virginica*.

Chaste tree develops into an upright, spreading form with medium-textured leaves and single or multiple stems. It is highly prized for its showy spikes of lavender flowers in late May and June. Small, dark gray berries develop in late summer and fall and remain until the following spring.

Often used as a specimen shrub or trained into a small tree by removing lower branches, the chaste tree is an excellent choice for use around pools, terraces, or patios. It is also interesting as an accent plant in a garden setting or as a shrub border to provide seasonal color before midsummer flowering shrubs come into bloom.

Grown in sun or partial shade, this shrub is tolerant of a wide range of soils and growing conditions and is free from most insects and diseases. A long-lived and trouble-free plant, the chaste tree is gaining increased popularity as a desirable shrub for contemporary garden and landscape use. Pink and white flowering varieties are also available.

Cherokee Rose (*Rosa laevigata*)

Native to China, the Cherokee rose is believed to have been introduced into the South by early Span-ish missionaries; it soon became widely naturalized throughout the Southeast where it can be seen growing along roadsides and woodland edges. The state flower of Georgia, this semi-evergreen climbing rose blooms in late March and April and produces occasional flowers in summer and fall. Measuring 2 to 3 inches across, its single white flowers have five petals and large yellow stamens.

Dark green foliage is produced on long, stout, arching stems containing thorns that are quite formidable in appearance. A vigorous climber, Cherokee rose should be given adequate space to grow. While more adaptable to naturalistic plantings, with regular pruning it can also be grown to great advantage in garden settings on fences, arbors, and small garden structures.

Tolerant of most soil conditions and free from insects and diseases, it will grow in both full sun and partial shade but blooms best in a location that provides sun. The Cherokee rose produces large, showy, pear-shaped fruit in autumn and winter.

Cherry Laurel (*Prunus caroliniana*)

Cherry laurel is a native shrub or small tree that grows from North Carolina to Texas and has been used in southern gardens since colonial times. Varying in height from 20 feet to 30 feet with a dense, upright habit of growth, this handsome plant has dark, glossy, evergreen leaves and small, white flowers that appear in early spring. Flowers are followed by inconspicuous, black-shiny berries.

The cherry laurel is useful for a variety of landscape purposes. Ideal as a tall screen, clipped hedge, or informal border planting, it can also be easily trained into a small decorative tree. The versatile nature of the cherry laurel makes it suitable as a specimen tree, formal hedge, or decorative container plant in a small garden. Its lustrous, medium-textured foliage can also be easily clipped into various shapes and forms to add a creative touch to a garden.

Growing both in sun or partial shade, the cherry laurel prefers a rich, well-drained, slightly alkaline soil. Free from most insects and diseases, it can be damaged by ice storms that often occur in the middle and upper South. Easy to transplant except in large sizes, the cherry laurel grows quite rapidly once it has become established.

Chinese Wisteria (*Wisteria sinensis*)

Chinese wisteria is a deciduous, woody vine native to China. It is an old-fashioned favorite grown throughout the Southeast for its fragrant, blue-violet flowers that occur in great profusion in spring on long pendulous clusters 6 to 12 inches long. Because flowers of Chinese wisteria occur on bare stems be-

tree by removing branches 3 to 4 feet up the stem and allowing the top branches to gracefully droop over the sides. Chinese wisteria also can be used as an espalier against a fence or wall.

Chinese wisteria is a vigorous growing vine. In order to restrict its growth and to keep it within bounds, it should be pruned annually—immediately after flowering or in winter. It does well in both sun and partial shade and prefers a deep, rich well-drained soil. Flowers may be sparse for the first few years or until the plant has become well established. Flowering can sometimes be improved by restricting fertilizer and water. Chinese wisteria is free from most insects and diseases and will give unequalled return for very little care.

Cleyera (*Cleyera japonica*)

Native to Japan, cleyera is a versatile evergreen shrub highly prized for its handsome glossy foliage that changes color with the seasons. Bright, copper-colored spring foliage gradually turns a dark, glossy green by summer, then changes to a deep wine-red in winter.

Cleyera is a medium- to slow-growing shrub that develops an upright, oval form and grows to a height of 6 to 8 feet. Small, creamy white, mildly fragrant flowers are produced in late spring, followed by a sparse number of dull red berries in fall.

With its upright form, cleyera is well suited for narrow, restricted spaces in small gardens and courtyards. Useful as a foundation plant, medium hedge, or specimen plant, it can also be grown in containers or pots for use around patios, terraces, or pools.

Grown both in sun or partial shade, cleyera prefers a well-drained, sandy soil with a medium to high moisture content. Selective pruning is recommended to maintain a desired shape and size. Cleyera is free

fore leaves begin to show, they create a breathtaking display. Foliage of the Chinese wisteria is lacy and fernlike with a delicate oriental appearance. Long, flat, velvety-covered seed pods that are light brown in color are produced during the summer and remain on the plant well into the fall.

Its use is ideal on walls and wrought-iron fences as well as arches, arbors, and porches—although its vigorous habit of growth may cause damage to wood and painted surfaces. It also can be trained as a small

from nearly all insects and diseases except for an occasional problem with leaf spot when plants are grown in poorly drained soils.

Common Hydrangea (*Hydrangea macrophylla*)

With its great profusion of colorful summer flowers, common hydrangea has long been an old-fashioned favorite of southern gardeners. Native to Japan, this deciduous, woody shrub with coarse-textured foliage and a mounding, compact form produces large, showy, flower clusters that last

for several weeks during May and June. Flowers can be either pink or blue depending on the alkalinity or acidity of the soil. Pink blossoms are produced in an alkaline soil and blue flowers in a more acidic one. Flowers, often measuring 6 to 8 inches across, generally remain on the plant several months after blooming.

Common hydrangea can be used effectively with other plants in a shrub border, or as a specimen or accent plant. It also can be grown in containers or tubs. With its somewhat stark and unattractive winter stem pattern, the common hydrangea should not be used in locations where an attractive year-round effect is desired. It may be grown both in sun or shade, although a greater number of flowers are produced when in a sunny location. It easily wilts and must be watered frequently during the summer months. Common hydrangea prefers a rich, moist, well-drained soil and an ample amount of fertilizer. Plants should be pruned annually immediately after flowering to maintain a desired shape and to encourage blooms the following season.

Coral Vine (*Antigonon leptopus*)

Coral vine is a fast-growing, medium- to coarse-textured, deciduous vine extremely popular in old city gardens in the lower South. A heat-loving, tuberous-rooted vine native to Mexico and Central America, it produces attractive clusters of rose-pink, heart-shaped flowers in summer and late fall, a valu-

able characteristic often overlooked. Bees are particularly attracted to its colorful flowers, especially during peak blooming periods. The flowers of coral vine also make excellent cut flowers. Climbing by tendrils, this is an ideal porch vine and does equally well on arbors, balconies, wire fences, masonry walls, and wooden structures.

Coral vine tolerates poor soils and is drought resistant. It will grow in sun or partial shade but blooms best in locations affording plenty of light. Producing vines that grow from 20 to 40 feet in one season, it should be cut back to ground level each year after frost. It will grow back rapidly the following spring to its original size.

Coral vine is excellent as a specimen in a small garden setting. Its late blooming, delicate pink flowers provide a colorful display at a time when most plants are long past their blooming periods.

Crape Myrtle (*Lagerstroemia indica*)

A native plant of China, crape myrtle is a large deciduous shrub or small tree widely grown throughout the South for its attractive flowers that bloom during most of the summer. Arriving in Europe around 1747, the crape myrtle was introduced into Charleston by André Michaux before the end of the eighteenth century.

Allowed to grow in its natural form, crape myrtle develops into a picturesque small tree that will reach an ultimate height of 20 to 25 feet. Its sculptured stems and exfoliating bark create an interesting effect particularly in the winter landscape. Crinkled, crepe-like flowers appear in late June and July, followed by prominent clusters of brown seed pods in late autumn and winter. Flowers range in color from white and pink to purple and watermelon red.

Highly versatile and adaptable to many landscape uses, crape myrtle is best used as a specimen where its distinctive character, sculptured trunks, and profusion of summer flowers can be seen and enjoyed.

Crape myrtle tolerates a wide range of soils and does best in a sunny location. If grown in shade, it becomes susceptible to mildew and sooty mold during periods of damp weather. Plants should be lightly pruned to maintain their overall shape and to remove seed heads that form in late summer and early fall.

Creeping Fig (*Ficus pumila*)

Native to Japan and China, creeping fig is a choice, medium-textured evergreen vine widely grown in the lower South to cover walls and masonry surfaces. In its early stage creeping fig sends out long, delicate branches. These create fernlike patterns of interesting tracery consisting of small heart-shaped leaves that lay flat, one over the other in a close fitting mat. As the plant matures, it develops long lateral shoots which hang free of the wall or growing surface. These shoots are covered with large, coarse-textured leaves that bear little resemblance to those found on younger plants. Annual pruning is recommended in order to reduce leaf density, to encourage young growth, and to control the development of older branches.

Creeping fig climbs by means of small aerial rootlets on stems which easily adhere to almost any surface. It grows well in sun or shade, tolerates a variety of soils, and is virtually free from all insects and diseases. Although susceptible to damage by severe cold or prolonged freezing, creeping fig generally can be depended

upon to send out new growth from its base each spring. Easily established and requiring very little space to grow, it is extremely useful in small gardens when planted in pockets of paved terraces and patios, in cracks between steps, and in narrow planting strips along walls and buildings. Creeping fig can cause damage to buildings and ornaments if its growth is allowed to go unchecked.

Evergreen Clematis (*Clematis armandi*)

Native to China, evergreen clematis is a handsome evergreen vine with beautiful, lanceolate leaves. This coarse-textured vine is worth growing for its foliage alone. In spring it produces large clusters of white, star-shaped flowers, 1 to 2½ inches wide, followed in late summer by long, plumy seed heads.

Evergreen clematis climbs by means of twisting petioles and often requires additional support when initially planted. It is useful on arbors, pergolas, walls, and fences, and is well suited for small gardens as an accent or specimen because of its spectacular display of rich, evergreen foliage and showy, fragrant flowers.

Slow to start, evergreen clematis will become a vigorous grower once established and will produce blooms when very young. Its only negative feature is a tendency to produce few leaves at the base of the vine. Growing to a height of 15 to 20 feet, it generally becomes dense with age and may require annual pruning. Pruning should occur immediately after blooming as flowers develop on foliage of the previous year.

Susceptible to severe cold and prolonged freezing, evergreen clematis will grow throughout the Southeast in protected locations. It prefers moist, well-drained soil and partial shade. For best results it should be left undisturbed once planted.

Fatshedera (*Fatshedera lizei*)

Fatshedera is an open, irregular, vine-like shrub that resulted from a cross between *Fatsia japonica*, a large leaf evergreen shrub from Japan, and common English ivy, *Herera helix*. Fatshedera is a popular foliage plant in the South and is characterized by large, glossy green leaves and long, weak stems that must be supported in some fashion, otherwise they will arch and bend to the ground. Spherical clusters of pale white flowers of little ornamental value develop in fall.

Fatshedera makes an excellent espalier plant or can be grown as an informal shrub. It is ideal for narrow planting strips against a garden wall or fence where its loose, natural tracery can be enjoyed. Fatshedera can also be grown in large tubs or planters for use as an accent plant around a terrace or patio.

Fatshedera grows best in full or partial shade and prefers a moist, fertile, well-drained soil. It is resistant to pest and diseases and is well suited to urban growing conditions. Susceptible to damage during cold winters, fatshedera should be planted in protected locations. With protection it can stand cold to zero degrees. As fatshedera has a tendency to develop long, bare stems, the growing tips of young plants should be pruned to encourage branching. Fatshedera is an excellent plant for a small garden where its bold evergreen leaves and interesting and distinct character can be enjoyed year around.

Fatsia (*Fatsia japonica*)

Native to Japan, fatsia is grown chiefly for its attractive, coarse-textured, evergreen foliage. Its deeply lobed, fan-like leaves are dark green and leathery in appearance. A very architectural plant, fatsia has a dense, rounded form with individual leaves that often reach a foot in diameter. It produces rounded clusters of creamy white flowers in the fall that last well into winter. Not extremely cold hardy, fatsia grows best in the lower South.

Suitable for courtyards, patios, terraces, planter boxes, and tubs, fatsia can also be used to great advantage in foundation plantings or as an accent plant to create bold and striking effects. Growing best in dense or partial shade, it will tolerate filtered light but burns if planted in locations with too much sun. Fatsia prefers a loose, well-drained soil rich in organic material. It should be pruned on an annual basis to keep plants low; otherwise, they will become tall and leggy with stalks reaching a height of 6 to 8 feet. Excellent for shady gardens as an accent or specimen plant, fatsia's dramatic, bold foliage adds an exotic, tropical touch to any garden, large or small.

Fig (*Ficus carica*)

A native of the Mediterranean region, the fig is one of the most popular fruit trees grown in the lower South. The Greeks and the Romans were great cultivators of figs and tradition has it that the Athenians loved figs so much that they forbade their export to other countries.

An upright, broad spreading deciduous shrub or small tree, the fig is chiefly grown for its fruits but is sometimes used as an attractive ornamental in pots or tubs to decorate patios and terraces. The fig develops large, coarse-textured, dark green leaves and pear-shaped, edible fruits that range in color from green to shades of brown depending on the variety grown. The cultivar most frequently found in Charleston gardens is *Celeste,* a small sweet fig that is one of the earliest to ripen. Birds are greatly attracted to the fruits of the fig and often inflict serious damage before they reach full maturity.

The fig requires ample space to grow and should never be planted closer than 25 feet apart. For best results plants should be located on the northern side of a building or wall where roots will receive partial shade and an abundant supply of moisture. In order to insure that plants are kept to a reasonable size and that fruit is accessible, plants should be pruned each year in a judicious manner. Severe winters often kill plants back to the ground but in most instances new growth will appear the following spring.

Flowering Dogwood (*Cornus florida*)

A popular flowering tree native to the eastern United States, the dogwood is beautiful in form, flower, and fruit. Well known to early botanists for its natural beauty, specimens were sent to England around 1731. Dogwood is characterized by a dense, upright shape when grown in sun and by a loose open form when planted in shade. Branches are usually horizontal and spreading with light green foliage that turns scarlet red in fall. Showy white flowers appear in spring before foliage appears. Clusters of bright red berries develop in late summer and last throughout fall and winter.

Flowering dogwood has many landscape uses, either as a small specimen tree or an accent plant in an informal or naturalistic setting. It makes an excellent choice for a patio, terrace, or small garden where it will provide year-round interest and enjoyment.

Dogwood grows best in partial to full shade and prefers a well-drained, acid soil with medium moisture and fertility. As dogwoods do not transplant well, it is best to plant small specimens that have a well-developed root system. Within recent years anthracnose, a serious leaf disease, has become a major problem for the dogwood. Several improved varieties of the native flowering dogwood are *White Cloud, Cloud 9,* and *Bonnie.*

Gardenia (*Gardenia jasminoides*)

Originally thought to be native to South Africa, the gardenia, or cape jasmine as it was initially known, was later found to have originated in China. The gardenia was named for Dr. Alexander Garden, a noted Charleston physician and botanist during the eighteenth century. Highly prized for its extremely fragrant flowers, the gardenia has been grown in southern gardens since colonial times.

An evergreen shrub with dark green, leathery leaves, gardenia will grow to a height of 4 to 6 feet and will ultimately develop into a large shrub with a rounded or oval form. The handsome, waxy-white, highly fragrant flowers of the gardenia bloom in late spring and early summer.

Well suited as a specimen plant near an entrance, walk, or patio where its fragrance can be enjoyed, gardenia can also be grown in pots or containers. While extremely hardy and reliable in the lower South, its use is questionable in areas where temperatures drop below twenty degrees.

Grown in both sun and partial shade, gardenia requires little attention besides mulching, fertilizing, and periodic watering during dry summer periods. Infestations of white fly and cottony cushion scale sometimes cause problems but can be controlled easily with periodic spraying.

Georgia Bark (*Pinckneya pubens*)

A native plant found only in the southeastern United States, the *Pinckneya* was first discovered by John and William Bartram in 1765 and later named by André Michaux for Charles Cotesworth Pinckney of Charleston, South Carolina. The *Pinckneya* usually grows along the marshy banks of streams and swamps where it develops into a large shrub or small tree that seldom exceeds 25 feet in height. Its leaves are 4 to 5 inches in length, light green in color with a downy surface underneath. Known as Georgia bark or fever tree, the bark of the plant was used by early inhabitants for treating malaria and other fevers.

The *Pinckneya* produces trumpet-shaped flowers that are white with longitudinal rose-colored stripes. These are surrounded by brilliant, pink, floral leaflets or bracts that occur in early summer resembling that of the familiar Christmas poinsettia.

While seldom seen in gardens today, the *Pinckneya* is one of the most attractive of our native woody plants and is useful as an accent or specimen plant for its unusual floral effect. For best results the *Pinckneya* should be planted along streams or ponds as it prefers moist soil in a location that is partially shaded.

Golden Wonder (*Cassia splendida*)

A native of South America, golden wonder is among the showiest of fall blooming plants producing flower clusters that resemble small golden but-

terflies. Characterized by a mounding habit of growth, this tender semi-evergreen shrub grows from 10 to 12 feet in height producing pinnately compound leaflets that range from 1 to 4 inches long and 2 inches wide. The spectacular bright yellow flowers of golden wonder are produced in late summer and fall at a time when few other plants are in bloom. Flowers are followed by cylindrical seed pods that have little aesthetic value.

Useful as an ornamental shrub either as a specimen or when grown in beds or borders, golden wonder is also attractive when combined in an evergreen planting. For best results plants need plenty of sun and a well-drained, fertile soil. Often damaged when winters are severe, golden wonder is best suited to a sheltered location that provides winter protection from cold north winds. Annual pruning of established plants is advised in order to insure an attractive shape and size. Another *Cassia* often found in Charleston gardens is *Cassia corymbosa*, a native of the West Indies that produces flowers throughout the summer and into the fall.

Hackberry (*Celtis laevigata*)

A native deciduous tree with a rounded or umbrella-like shape, the hackberry was referred to by early naturalists as the unknown wood. One of the most dependable trees for urban planting in the lower South, the hackberry is characterized by pendulous branches, smooth gray bark, and fine-textured foliage that is a beautiful olive-green in spring and yellow in fall. The hackberry produces small red-brown berries which generally go unnoticed amid heavy midsummer foliage but are much appreciated and enjoyed by birds.

A hardy, fast-growing tree, the hackberry is relatively long lived and is extremely useful for street tree planting or as a shade tree for residential grounds. Its handsome pattern of branches makes it particularly attractive and striking in the winter landscape. The hackberry's dense canopy of leaves and its shallow root system make it difficult for grass or shrubs to grow underneath older specimens.

Easily grown in poor soils, the hackberry will tolerate drought, alkaline soils, and difficult urban conditions. Seldom available in nurseries, plants are generally obtained from the woods or as volunteers which occur from seed near older trees.

Harland Boxwood (*Buxus harlandii*)

Native to Japan, Harland boxwood is a small, compact evergreen shrub used throughout the South—particularly in formal gardens. It is distinguished from other types of boxwood by its inverted pyramid shape, rounded top, and narrow base, as well as its long, thin, dark green leaves.

Excellent as a specimen or accent plant, Harland boxwood is frequently used as a low clipped hedge. When used in this manner, plants are usually spaced 12 inches apart and are regularly clipped to maintain a desired height and form.

Growing both in sun or shade, Harland boxwood prefers moist, fertile, well-drained soil. A shallow root system precludes cultivation around the base of the plant. Pruning should occur in late winter before new spring growth appears. Proper feeding, watering, spraying, and pruning are necessary to maintain this plant at its best. Harland boxwood is useful in the small garden as a specimen plant to create a strong focal point or as a low hedge to define space and articulate a design.

Indian Hawthorn (*Raphiolepis indica*)

A native of southern China, Indian hawthorn is a slow-growing evergreen shrub that is widely planted in the lower South. Exceptional in foliage, flower, and fruit, this highly versatile shrub usually grows no more than 4 feet in height. The overall form of Indian hawthorn is mounding to spreading with a distinctive dramatic appearance. Its dark green, leathery leaves often take on a purplish cast in winter especially when planted in open, exposed locations. Profuse clusters of dark rosy-pink to white flowers appear in April with intermittent blossoms occurring throughout the summer and fall. Flowers are followed in late autumn by showy blue-black fruits.

Indian hawthorn makes an excellent informal hedge and can be combined with low growing shrubs in beds, borders, or foundation plantings. Also useful in containers, this highly decorative plant makes an attractive addition to patios, terraces, and entrance areas. Both drought and salt tolerant, Indian hawthorn is easy to grow in almost any location where there is adequate drainage, fertile soil, and several hours of direct sunlight. To keep plants to a desired size, pruning should occur soon after plants have bloomed in early spring. Several of the more popular cultivars include *Rosea, Enchantress,* and *Fascination.*

Japanese Anise (*Illicium anisatum*)

Native to Japan, Japanese anise is an excellent, broad-leaved evergreen shrub commonly grown in old gardens of the South for its attractive and aromatic foliage. Growing to a height of 10 to 12 feet, this somewhat massive shrub develops an upright, rounded form that is open and spreading in character.

Large, dark olive-green, leathery leaves—2 to 3 inches long—emit a distinct aniselike smell when crushed or broken. Young leaves grow in an upright habit, almost flat against the stem at a forty-five-degree angle; they become more relaxed and less rigid with age. Small, yellow-green flowers develop in the summer, followed by inconspicuous brown fruit in the fall.

Ideal as an unclipped hedge or screen for privacy and enclosure, Japanese anise is also useful in informal, naturalistic plantings. It can be used effectively as a foundation plant for large buildings or as an espalier against a wall.

Adaptable to both sun and partial shade, it becomes more open when grown in shady locations or as an understory shrub. Japanese anise tolerates a variety of soils and growing conditions as long as it receives adequate drainage and a moderate amount of moisture. Free from pests and diseases, it should be judiciously pruned and never clipped. Ranked as one of the best shrubs in its size group, once established Japanese anise is extremely dependable and trouble-free.

Japanese Boxwood (*Buxus microphylla* var. *japonica*)

A native of Japan, Japanese boxwood is commonly used in gardens of the lower South as a substitute for common boxwood (*Buxus sempervirens*) and dwarf English or edging box (*Buxus sempervirens* var. *suffruticosa*) which are intolerant of the intense summer heat and high humidity of the coastal plain. Similar in shape and overall character to common boxwood, Japanese boxwood is ideally suited for use in both formal and informal garden designs.

A compact, oval-shaped, evergreen shrub, Japanese boxwood has fine-textured foliage with rounded leaves, approximately 1 inch long. Leaves are yellow-green but turn bronze-brown during cold winters or when grown in exposed, sunny locations. Useful as a foundation or specimen plant, Japanese boxwood is ideal as a low clipped evergreen hedge that can be pruned and shaped into a variety of heights and forms. It is also suitable for planting in containers or pots for use around patios, pools, or entrances.

Tolerant of sun or partial shade, Japanese boxwood will grow in most any soil as long as it is reasonably well drained. Because it is relatively shallow rooted, cultivation should be kept to a minimum around the base of individual plants. While resistant to most insects and diseases, red spider may at times become a problem. Moderate pruning is required to keep plants to a desired height and form.

Japanese Viburnum (*Viburnum japonicum*)

A native of Japan, Japanese viburnum is a large, lustrous-leaved, evergreen shrub widely grown throughout the lower and middle South for its glossy foliage and strong pyramidal form. Often listed as *Viburnum macrophyllum,* this is an excellent plant for the coastal plains because of its hardiness and tolerance of intense summer heat and high humidity.

A large, coarse-textured plant with slender, glossy, dark green leaves, measuring 3 to 6 inches long, Japanese viburnum develops a form that is upright and erect with multiple stems. Reaching a height of 8 to 10 feet, it is often planted in locations that will not accommodate its ultimate size. Creamy white and mildly fragrant flower clusters develop in late May, followed by a sparse number of bright red fruits in late summer and early fall.

With its upright habit of growth, Japanese viburnum makes an excellent screen or hedge when planted approximately 4 feet apart. Useful as a large foundation shrub or accent plant, it also can be trained into a handsome small tree by selectively pruning lower branches. It can be grown in large containers or pots as a specimen plant when an upright form and coarse-textured effect is desired.

Cold hardy into the upper South, Japanese viburnum thrives in moist, fertile, well-drained soils in either full sun or partial shade. It is resistant to most insects and plant diseases.

Japanese Yew (*Podocarpus macrophyllus*)

A native of Japan, Japanese yew is unique in leaf shape, plant form, and growth habit when compared to other evergreen shrubs grown in the South. Its characteristic columnar form and dark green, fine-textured foliage has a distinctive oriental character that adds an exotic touch to a garden or landscape design.

Growing to a height of 10 to 15 feet, this large evergreen shrub can be used as a foundation plant, clipped hedge, container plant, or as an espalier against a wall or fence. When grown in the sun, Japanese yew takes on a very dense, compact form as compared to a loose open shape when planted in shade. It responds well to pruning and is useful in small narrow spaces. Old, mature plants can be easily pruned into small evergreen trees. The Japanese yew is an excellent plant for the small garden because of its slow rate of growth, adaptability to shearing, and ability to grow in locations with limited space.

Preferring a rich, well-drained soil with medium to high moisture content, Japanese yew is totally free from insects and plant diseases. It is also tolerant of salt and drought.

Jerusalem Thorn (*Parkinsonia aculeata*)

A native plant of the West Indies and tropical America, Jerusalem thorn is a small deciduous tree suitable only for the lower South. Unique in form, flower, and foliage, it will grow to a height of 25 to 30 feet. Jerusalem thorn has a loose, irregular, and unpredictable shape with thin, wiry branches pendulous in form. It has small, fine-textured leaves that have a distinct fern-like appear-

ance. Branches remain green year around, giving an evergreen appearance even after the loss of the small, yellow-green leaves in the fall. Profuse, yellow pea-like flowers appear in late spring and occur intermittently throughout the summer. Jerusalem thorn is an excellent choice for a location where extremes of heat and drought are problems. It is ideal for a small garden when planted against a wall where its drooping branches will create an interesting pattern against a solid surface.

It does best when planted in a sunny location in loose, well-drained soils. Free from insects and diseases, it is tolerant of salt and therefore a good selection for beachside plantings. Generally considered a short-lived tree, Jerusalem thorn should be planted in areas where it can be replaced easily without major loss to a design.

Kurume Azalea (*Azalea obtusum*)

Native to Japan, kurume azaleas are extremely popular in southern gardens for their extravagant display of spring flowers. Hardier than Indian azaleas, kurume azaleas have smaller leaves and flowers and develop a more compact habit of growth. Their brightly colored blossoms and low, spreading form are particularly useful for small gardens.

The fine-textured, dark green foliage of some kurume azaleas turns wine-red during the winter months, especially when grown in exposed locations. Flowers bloom in early spring and range in color from white to pink, rose, or red. Special care should be taken when combining varieties to avoid clashing color combinations.

Excellent for foundation plantings or for use around patios, terraces, or pools, kurume azaleas are also attractive in natural areas when planted in drifts or informal masses.

Plants grow best in fertile, moist, well-drained, and acid soil. They need a permanent mulch of pine straw or leaves and, following flowering, benefit from an annual application of azalea fertilizer. Growing both in sun and shade, they do best in locations that provide filtered sunlight. Kurume azaleas respond well to clipping and can be maintained as low, spreading shrubs. Their chief pests and problems include the mealy bug, red spider mite, and root rot. Commonly grown varieties include Coral Bells, Snow, Pink Pearl, and Christmas Cheer.

Lady Banksia Rose (*Rosa banksiae*)

Native to China, Lady Banksia rose is a thornless, semi-evergreen, climbing rose that blooms in late spring. Popular throughout the Southeast, this vigorous, fast-growing plant is one of the earliest climbing roses to flower. Lady Banksia rose can be found in four main forms: white or yellow and single or double. The double flowering, yellowing variety

is the most popular, producing a profusion of fragrant, showy flowers that are a traditional feature in many southern gardens.

Its mounding, shrub-like habit of growth requires sturdy support and ample space to accommodate the sprawling, arching shoots that are characteristic of this plant. Often trained on fences, walls, and arbors, it frequently is used to screen unsightly views or to cover small buildings or garden structures.

In addition to annual pruning, Lady Banksia rose should be clipped several times a season to contain its vigorous growth. Not particular about soil, it does best in sunny locations if provided ample space to grow. A long-lived plant, Lady Banksia rose is relatively free of most insects and diseases.

Laurustinus (*Viburnum tinus*)

Native to the Mediterranean region, laurustinus is a handsome evergreen shrub that was introduced into England around 1560. Grown in American gardens since colonial times, this versatile, medium-textured shrub is considered an indispensable plant in many southern gardens. Reaching a height of 7 to 10 feet, laurustinus produces dark lustrous green leaves and small pinkish to white flowers in clusters that are approximately 3 inches across. Flowers occur in late winter and spring and are followed in summer and early fall, by blue-black, metallic fruit that generally persists for long periods of time.

Ideal for mass plantings, screens, or as background material for a shrub border, laurustinus also makes an excellent hedge which can go unclipped for several years and still retain an excellent shape and form.

Growing best in fertile, well-drained soil in locations providing full sun or partial shade, laurustinus prefers older, well-established sites with porous soils. A relatively drought-resistant shrub, plants should be watered sparingly in late summer to restrict growth which may be winter killed and remain unsightly until spring. Laurustinus is generally free from insects and diseases and as a rule is a long-lived shrub.

Live Oak (*Quercus virginiana*)

The live oak is a native evergreen tree found growing in the southern coastal plain from Virginia to Florida. It is characterized by a short trunk and a massive, mounding form with horizontal branches that arch to the ground and then turn upward again. At maturity the live oak may reach a height of 120 feet and obtain a spread of 75 feet. The live oak is a dramatic tree because of its sheer size and pictur-

esque shape. Foliage of the live oak is medium in texture with leaves that are blue-green, except in spring when new growth is an attractive yellow-green color. Acorns form in clusters on short, multiple stems. Spanish moss is often found growing in the branches of the live oak, giving it a mystical appearance.

The live oak is a magnificent, long-lived specimen tree ideal for large open areas. It is also useful as a street tree where space is not restricted and mature branches do not interfere with circulation and traffic flow. Its ultimate size at maturity requires that the live oak be used with great caution in any garden, either large or small.

Growing best in full sun, the live oak will tolerate a variety of soil conditions and is virtually disease-free. Salt tolerant, it is useful for coastal plantings or in areas affected by salt spray. Easy to transplant, even in large sizes, live oak is a versatile tree often referred to as the matriarch of the South.

Loquat (*Eriobotrya japonica*)

Native to China and Japan, loquat is an attractive, broadleaf evergreen with a dense, rounded shape and a lush, tropical appearance. It develops into a large shrub or multi-stem, small tree that will grow to an ultimate height of 15 to 20 feet.

Its stiff, leathery leaves are dark green on top and gray-green with a brown feltlike covering on the undersides. Leaves vary in length from 5 to 10 inches and are often clustered around the tips of branches forming large coarse-textured rosettes. Clusters of creamy white, fragrant flowers emerge in late fall, followed by small, orange, pear-shaped, edible fruit which can be eaten raw, steamed, or used in preserves. Fruit generally develops only on plants grown in the lower South. Loquat can be used as a specimen, a background plant, or as a screen. It is often substituted for southern magnolia where space is limited.

Loquat grows best in full sun or light shade and in fertile, loamy, and well-drained soil. Generally pest-free, it is susceptible to fire blight. Loquat is one of the few evergreen trees highly adaptable to small spaces. It can successfully be used as a small tree, grown in planters, or espaliered against a wall.

Mimosa (*Albizia julibrissin*)

Native to Asia, mimosa, or silk tree, as it is sometimes called, was introduced into South Carolina by André Michaux around the end of the eighteenth century. Since that time it has become naturalized along the eastern coast as far north as Philadelphia. William Bartram, in a letter to Thomas Jefferson, describes the graceful mimosa as "a native of Persia and Armenia, lately brought to us by the celebrated Michaux the Elder." The genus name, sometimes spelled *Albizzia*, commemorates a well-known Italian naturalist, Filippo degli Albizzi, who is credited with introducing the tree into Italy from Persia or Central China.

Mimosa is a deciduous tree with a broad, spreading picturesque form. It produces graceful, lacy leaves and delicate, pink pompom-like flowers that are borne in profusion during late May and June. Flowers are followed by flat, papery brown seed pods, 4 to 6 inches long, that remain on the tree well into winter. A fast-growing tree, mimosa is relatively short lived and can be somewhat messy due to falling flowers, sap, and seeds.

Reaching a height of 30 to 40 feet, the mimosa is generally used as a specimen tree or as an accent plant in a landscape setting. Because the low-branching habit of the mimosa can create problems with pedestrian circulation, lower branches are often pruned up to form a high-branched, umbrella-like canopy. While the mimosa is susceptible to webworms and mimosa wilt disease, several new wilt resistant strains have been developed under the trade names of *Charlotte* and *Tryon*.

Morning Glory (*Ipomoea purpurea*)

A native of tropical America, morning glory is a fast-growing, annual vine widely grown throughout the southeastern United States. Climbing by twisting stems, morning glory produces dark green, heart-shaped leaves and a magnificent display of large, trumpet-shaped flowers which can be obtained in shades of purple, blue, scarlet, crimson, and pink. Flowers bloom from midsummer to fall—opening in early morning and fading by mid-afternoon. Older varieties usually reseed and return year after year.

Useful as a quick, temporary screen for porches, trellises, arbors, posts, and fences, it also makes an ideal ground cover for roadside plantings and banks. When used in a garden setting, morning glory should be planted in a location where its decorative flowers can be enjoyed and its rampant

growth easily contained.

For best results, morning glory should be planted in a rich, loose, well-drained soil and a bright sunny location. Seeds can be sown several times a season to insure a continuous display of blooms. Plants should be removed once the flowering season is over. An easy to grow, serviceable vine, morning glory is generally trouble-free except for an occasional infestation of aphids which can be controlled easily by spraying.

Oleander (*Nerium oleander*)

Oleander is a popular evergreen shrub native to the Mediterranean region and widely grown throughout the South. Reaching a height of 10 to 15 feet, it develops an upright, rounded form with multi-

canelike stems and leathery, gray-green leaves. Showy clusters of fragrant flowers, ranging in color from white to pink to red, appear throughout the summer. Both single and double flowering varieties are available.

Ideally suited for use as a specimen or as a free-form hedge, oleander can also be grown effectively in containers and tubs as an accent plant. It will tolerate a variety of soils and grows best in full sun. Extremely heat and drought resistant, it does well in urban areas. It is tolerant of salt spray and is useful in beachside plantings.

One drawback of this beautiful and versatile ornamental shrub is that all parts are poisonous if eaten. Resistant to nearly all insects, it is sometimes infested with scale, evidenced by a sooty coating on the leaves. When damaged by severe cold, branches should be cut back to ground level in late winter before new growth appears.

Palmetto (*Sabal palmetto*)

The palmetto is a native palm found growing in coastal areas from North Carolina to Florida along marshes, pinelands, and beachfront areas. Its fan-shaped foliage and tall vertical trunks add a tropical

and picturesque character to the coastal landscape. Palmetto logs were used in the construction of early forts that protected Charleston's harbor against attacks by the British during the Revolutionary War. The palmetto is the state tree of South Carolina.

The palmetto reaches a height of 40 to 50 feet, developing a rounded canopy of coarse-textured foliage that occurs at the top of a single, branchless trunk.

Producing no flowers or fruit of any consequence, the palmetto is useful for its distinctive character and ability to adapt to a variety of locations.

Often used as a street tree or as a specimen in a landscape scheme, the palmetto provides an interesting shadow pattern against a solid surface and creates a strong vertical element effective in defining and articulating an outdoor space. Growing in both sun and shade, it will tolerate a variety of soils and can be easily transplanted even in large sizes.

Pittosporum (*Pittosporum tobira*)

A native of China and Japan, pittosporum is grown throughout the lower South and is regarded by many southern gardeners as one of the most valuable and versatile plants of the region. An excellent,

long-lived evergreen shrub, it produces handsome foliage consisting of rosettes of dark green, leathery leaves. Clusters of creamy white to pale yellow waxy flowers, with a fragrance similar to orange blossoms, develop in April and May.

Pittosporum's dense, spreading, or horizontal form proves ideal for foundation plantings, informal screens, and clipped hedges. It also can be grown effectively in containers and pots. Older plants can be pruned into attractive multi-stem specimens.

Tolerant of both full sun and partial shade, pittosporum will grow in a variety of soils. It should be selectively pruned to insure an interesting shape and form. Generally quite healthy and free of insects and disease, it is susceptible to occasional in-festations of aphids and cottony cushion scale. Salt tolerant, it can be safely used in seaside locations. Pittosporum is vulnerable to freeze damage if temperatures drop into the mid-teens.

Pomegranate (*Punica granatum*)

Native to southern Asia and grown since ancient times for its decorative flowers and edible fruit, the pomegranate is a favorite deciduous shrub of old southern gardens. Reaching a maximum height of 10 to 15 feet, the pomegranate produces shiny, grey-green leaves that are copper color in spring and yellow in fall. Single or double, carnation-like flowers develop in May and June. Double flowering varieties seldom produce good fruit. Flowers of the pomegranate are typically orange scarlet in color, although white, yellow, and variegated varieties are available.

Often used as a specimen because of its colorful flowers and decorative fruit, the pomegranate can be trained into an attractive, small, multi-stemmed tree by removing lower stems and branches. It is also useful as a high hedge when plants are closely spaced and properly pruned.

Growing well in full sun or partial shade, the pomegranate prefers a moist, well-drained, slightly acidic soil. A long-lived, relatively slow growing shrub, it is free from pests and diseases.

Pyracantha (*Pyracantha coccinea*)

Native to southern Europe and Western Asia, pyracantha is an extremely popular shrub grown throughout the South for its brilliant display of scarlet berries in autumn and winter. Often trained as an espalier on walls and fences, pyracantha's attractive foliage and colorful fall berries add seasonal interest to many southern gardens and landscapes.

An upright, spreading evergreen shrub with a distinctive horizontal branching habit, pyracantha reaches a maximum height of 10 to 12 feet. Clusters of mildly fragrant, small, white flowers appear in late spring, followed in the fall by heavy bunches of bright red fruit that often last well into the winter season.

Pyracantha is useful in a shrub border as a screen or a specimen plant. Its ability to tolerate severe pruning, coupled with its somewhat vine-like habit of growth, make it especially adaptable as an espalier in confined or restricted garden spaces.

Pyracantha will tolerate a variety of soils but for best results requires good drainage and a sunny location. Plants should be pruned annually to maintain a desired shape. Since berries occur on two-year-old wood, it is essential that care be taken to preserve some of the previous year's foliage. While pyracantha is a highly desirable and versatile plant, it is not without problems. Its susceptibility to scale, lacebug, and fire blight require that special care be provided to insure that it maintains an attractive appearance.

Sasanqua (*Camellia sasanqua*)

Native to China and Japan, the sasanqua is a popular broadleaf evergreen highly prized for its attractive foliage and late autumn-flowering, camellia-like flowers. While the flowers of the sasanqua resemble the common camellia, the plant has a distinctive character and identity all its own. Sasanquas have a more open, informal, bushier habit of growth and generally reach a height of 8 to 10 feet.

The foliage of the sasanqua is glossy, dark green, and somewhat narrower than that of *Camellia japonica*. Flowers can be single or double and bloom in late fall or early winter, adding interest to the garden when few other shrubs are in bloom. Flowers range in color from white, rose, and pink to shades of red.

Useful as a high, upright hedge or screen or as large foundation shrub, the sasanqua also makes an excellent espalier against a wall, fence, or trellis—particularly in a courtyard or small garden space. Older specimens can be easily trained into small multi-stem trees by removing lower branches.

Growing both in sun or shade, the sasanqua prefers a moist, well-drained, slightly acidic soil. It is generally free from most insects and diseases, except scale which requires periodic spraying. Commonly grown varieties include *Cleopatra*, *Maiden's Blush*, *Gulf Breeze*, and *Mine-No-Yuki*.

Southern Indian Azalea (*Azalea indica*)

Native to China and Japan, Indian azaleas found their way into Europe at a time when the Orient was known as India or the Indies—thus the name Indian azalea was derived. Indian azaleas were later introduced into the United States as hybrids developed in England and Belgium and were first grown in the North in greenhouse and later in the South as outdoor plants, with the first significant plantings occurring at Magnolia Gardens around 1843. They since have been used extensively in Southern gardens for their evergreen foliage and magnificent display of spring flowers which vary in size from 2 to $3^1/_2$ inches across. Blooms last for several weeks and include a variety of colors ranging from white, pink, and rose to salmon, magenta, and orange.

Medium in texture with a broad spreading or mounding form, Indian azaleas are ideal for use as specimen plants, mass plantings, or naturalized drifts. They grow rapidly to a height of 6 to 10 feet with a spread of equal dimensions. Grown both in sun or shade, they should be planted in loose, well-drained, acidic soils with a medium to high moisture content. For best results plants should be hand pruned. As southern Indian azaleas have a shallow root system, they are easily transplanted during winter months when plants are in a dormant stage.

While many varieties of southern Indian azaleas are available, several that are favorites in southern gardens include *George L. Taber* (pink with lavender markings), *Mrs. G. G. Gerbing* (large white), *Pride of Mobile* (deep rose pink), and *Formosa* (magenta).

Southern Magnolia (*Magnolia grandiflora*)

Described in 1757 by Dr. Alexander Garden of Charleston as the finest and most superb evergreen tree that the earth produced, the southern magnolia was recognized by many early botanists for its outstanding beauty and ornamental value. A native plant that grows from North Carolina to Texas, southern magnolia reaches a maximum height of 60 to 90 feet and develops an upright, oval form.

Lush evergreen foliage and highly fragrant flowers are distinctive features of this versatile plant. Its long, leathery leaves are glossy, dark green on top and rusty brown beneath. Large, white flowers, measuring 6 to 10 inches across, appear in late spring and early summer. These are followed by the devel-

ing space is restricted or confined.

Tolerant of a wide range of growing conditions, southern magnolia prefers sun or partial shade, medium moisture, and an acidic soil. Free from most diseases and insect pests, it is generally a long-lived and trouble-free plant. Several small growing varieties, including *Little Gem,* are recommended for gardens with limited space.

Star Jasmine (*Trachelospermum jasminoides*)

Star jasmine, or Confederate jasmine, as it is commonly referred to in Charleston, is a popular vine highly prized in southern gardens for its evergreen foliage and wonderfully fragrant flowers. A native of China, this moderate growing vine produces white, star-shaped flowers that bloom in great profusion in late spring and early summer. Ideal for pergolas, porches, arbors, fences, and garden structures, star jasmine is an exceptionally desirable vine with graceful, delicate stems that twine to create interesting  tracery and dense screens of compact foliage. When star jasmine is grown against a wall or around a doorway, a wire or metal frame is required to provide support.

While slow to start, once established star jasmine will become a vigorous grower requiring annual

opment of cylindrical cones with bright red seeds in the fall.

Southern magnolia is a superb specimen tree well suited for large open areas. Magnolias are at their best when their lower branches are allowed to grow to the ground, eliminating the need for removal of litter and leaves. Excellent as an evergreen screen or visual barrier, the southern magnolia is surprisingly adaptable as an espalier for large walls or building surfaces, even when plant-

pruning to control its size and to increase the number of flowers the following season. Often damaged during severe winters, star jasmine benefits from a protected or sheltered location. Thriving in full sun or partial shade, it grows best in moist, well-drained soil. While normally grown as a vine, star jasmine also makes an excellent ground cover.

Sweet Orange (*Citrus sinensis*)

Originating in subtropical and tropical Asia and the Malay Archipelago, oranges are among the oldest cultivated fruit, first being recorded in Chinese writing as early as 500 B.C. Introduced into the western hemisphere by Columbus in 1493, oranges were grown in Charleston during the eighteenth century and were frequently listed among the products exported from the colony. Oranges are still grown in Charleston gardens today for their fruit and as a decorative ornamental.

Oranges fall within three major categories: sweet oranges (*Citrus sinensis*), sour oranges (*Citrus aurantium*), and mandarins (*Citrus reticulata*), each having many varieties. Of the three types, the sweet orange is the most commonly grown in the lower South as a small evergreen tree or as an attractive ornamental for pot cultivation for use on patios, terraces, and in courtyards.

Low-branched with a rounded crown and dense evergreen foliage, the sweet orange produces white, waxy, highly fragrant flowers in March and April. These are followed in December by yellow-orange, round to oval shaped, edible fruit. Susceptible to cold, the sweet orange should be planted in a protected location with a southern or southeastern orientation or in pots which can be moved inside during periods of winter freezes.

Plants perform best in well-drained, slightly acid to neutral loamy soil. Established plants should be fertilized at intervals from late winter to early fall with a general fertilizer high in nitrogen. Subject to a large number of insects and diseases, sweet oranges should be sprayed several times during the warm months of the year.

Sweet Shrub (*Calycanthus floridus*)

A native deciduous shrub that grows in the southeastern United States from Virginia to Florida, sweet shrub or Carolina allspice as it is often called, was first sent to England in 1726 and has been used in American gardens since colonial times for its fragrant flowers and aromatic foliage.

A coarse-textured plant with an upright oval form and multiple stems, sweet shrub grows naturally in moist woodland areas where it reaches a height of 6 to 8 feet. Its leaves are dark green on top, gray-green underneath, and aromatic when crushed or dried. Golden yellow foliage is produced in the fall. Dull, reddish brown flowers, measuring 2 inches across, appear in April and May. These small, inconspicuous flowers produce a spicy aroma similar to strawberries or ripened fruit.

Ideal for naturalistic and mass plantings or for a mixed shrub border, sweet shrub is also useful as a foundation plant. While once commonly found in early gardens, sweet shrub remains desirable for contemporary use.

Growing both in sun and partial shade, sweet shrub tolerates a variety of soils and growing conditions. It is particularly adaptable to poorly drained soils. Generally trouble-free and disease resistant, it should be pruned periodically to remove old wood and to maintain a desired height and form.

Sweetbay Magnolia (*Magnolia virginiana*)

The sweetbay magnolia is a small, upright native tree found growing along the coastal areas of the eastern United States. Sent to England in 1688 by John Bannister, an English missionary, the sweetbay has the distinction of being the first magnolia introduced to the British Isles from America. A member of the magnolia family, the sweetbay is often referred to as swamp magnolia, white bay, and swamp laurel. Thomas Jefferson in *Notes on the State of Virginia*, classified the native sweetbay as an ornamental.

Growing to a height of 20 to 30 feet, the sweetbay magnolia is often multi-trunk with smooth, gray bark. Small, white flowers, 2 to 3 inches across, appear in late spring and early summer. These waxy, magnolia-like blossoms have a remarkably penetrating fragrance and can be detected at a considerable distance if the wind is favorable. The aromatic, almost evergreen foliage is green on top and gray or silvery-green on the undersides. When blown by the wind, the leaves create an interesting effect as they sparkle and glitter in the breeze.

Adaptable to normal garden conditions, the sweetbay magnolia is problem- and disease-free and can be grown easily in both sun and shade. The upright, narrow growth habit of the sweetbay magnolia makes it ideal as a small specimen tree for gardens with limited space.

Tallow Tree (*Sapium sebiferum*)

Native to China and Japan, tallow tree is grown throughout the lower South and has become naturalized over much of the coastal region. Deriving its name from the waxy, white seeds from which the Chinese extract a material for making candles, it is also referred to by many Charlestonians as the popcorn tree because of its white, popcorn-like fruit that lasts well into the winter months.

A deciduous tree that reaches a maximum height of 35 to 40 feet, tallow tree develops a somewhat open and irregular form. In the fall its medium green foliage turns brilliant red, yellow, or purple. Small, yellow, drooping spikes develop in late spring followed by small seed pods which can become a maintenance problem when this tree is planted along walks and other paved surfaces.

Often used in residential plantings for quick shade and brilliant, reliable fall foliage, tallow tree is extremely hardy and dependable even when grown under adverse conditions. It is useful as a lawn tree where filtered light is needed to sustain grass or in difficult locations where limited space requires its upright, vertical form.

Able to grow in full sun or partial shade, the tallow tree requires no special soil or care and is resistant to most insects and plant diseases. While easy to establish and grow, it unfortunately is rather a short-lived tree.

Tea Olive (*Osmanthus fragrans*)

A native plant of Asia, tea olive is a favorite in Southern gardens. Its tiny, white flowers bloom from late autumn to early spring and produce a delightful and unforgettable fragrance, often described as one of the greatest pleasures of a Southern garden. Tea olive was introduced into the South by André Michaux before the end of the eighteenth century.

susceptible to damage during severe winters and benefits from a protected location. When harmed by the cold, it should be judiciously pruned to insure that its natural shape is preserved and that undamaged wood is retained.

Trumpet Honeysuckle (*Lonicera sempervirens*)

Trumpet honeysuckle is a native American vine listed by Thomas Jefferson as an ornamental in 1781 and often referred to in the writings of many prominent botanists and naturalists during colonial times. A semi-evergreen, twining vine with many wiry stems, trumpet honeysuckle is extremely hardy and reliable. Attractive to hummingbirds and butterflies, showy clusters of orange-red, trumpet-shaped flowers bloom in midspring and summer. Orange to scarlet berries are produced in late summer and fall.

Trumpet honeysuckle is a moderate to vigorous grower, producing vines 15 to 20 feet long. Unlike the Japanese honeysuckle (*Lonicera japonica*), it is easy to control. An excellent vine for the small garden, it is ideal for creating a point of interest on a fence, lamppost, mailbox, balustrade, or other architectural feature.

Grown both in sun and shade, trumpet honeysuckle tolerates a wide range of soils and will withstand drought conditions. With age it develops a heavy canopy and often becomes leggy at the base. Generally free from most diseases and insects, it is a favorite of

A large evergreen shrub with an upright, oval form and finely serrated leaves, tea olive is often used as a foundation plant or as a specimen near an entrance, walk, or terrace where its perfumed fragrance can best be enjoyed. It is also a desirable plant for tubs or containers for use on patios and decks.

Adaptable to both sun and partial shade, tea olive is tolerant of most growing conditions, except heavy clay soils. Resistant to most insects and diseases, it is

aphids at certain seasons, but these easily can be controlled with periodic spraying.

Trumpet Vine (*Campsis radicans*)

Often referred to as trumpet vine, trumpet creeper, or cow-itch vine, this native southeastern deciduous vine was first listed by early botanists as *Bignonia radicans* and was sent to England as early as 1640. Often ignored as an ornamental in the South because of its rampant growth in fields, pastures, and roadsides, trumpet vine can become a spectacular addition to any garden if given a location with sufficient light and ample space to grow.

Throughout the summer the trumpet vine produces clusters of orange-red, trumpet-shaped flowers that are particularly attractive to hummingbirds. Cigar-shaped seed pods, 5 to 6 inches long, develop in late summer and fall, creating interesting winter patterns against walls and fences. Adhering to stone and wood by means of small aerial rootlets, this coarse-textured vine generally requires additional support because of its shrubby nature and heavy mounding foliage.

Trumpet vine will grow to a height of 20 to 30 feet and will tolerate a variety of soil conditions. It is extremely heat and drought resistant, free from most diseases and insects, and extremely long lived. It is an excellent choice for masonry walls or for use on arbors for shade. Improved hybrids include: *Crimson Trumpet*, notable for its clusters of pure glowing red flowers; *Madame Galen*, with flowers that are a rich apricot-tinted orange and fine dark green foliage; and *Flava*, a yellow trumpeted variety that produces clusters of bright apricot flowers.

Wax-Leaf Ligustrum (*Ligustrum japonicum*)

Wax-leaf ligustrum is a desirable, broadleaf evergreen shrub used extensively in southern gardens for its highly versatile and durable qualities. Native to Japan, this fast-growing, medium-textured shrub with glossy, dark green leaves produces showy clusters of small white flowers in late spring that emit a strong, pungent fragrance. Flowers are followed by a profusion of blue-black berries that appear in late fall and winter and attract birds.

Traditionally used as a clipped evergreen hedge or a reliable foundation plant, wax-leaf ligustrum is also useful as background material or as an informal screen. It can be trained into a small multi-stem tree that will reach a height of 10 to 15 feet. It can also be grown in tubs or containers and effectively trained into topiary. Wax-leaf ligustrum is an excellent plant for the small garden when trained into a small multi-stem tree and used as a focal point to highlight its distinctive sculptural form.

A highly dependable plant that tolerates adverse growing conditions and requires very little care, wax-leaf ligustrum is an excellent, trouble-free, long-lived plant. Growing best in sun or partial shade, it tolerates heat, drought, and salt but demands well-drained soils. Generally resistant to most insects and diseases, it is occasionally infested with white flies or scale.

Yaupon Holly (*Ilex vomitoria*)

Yaupon holly is a native evergreen of the southeastern United States. Its leaves contain a high level of caffeine and were used by American Indians to concoct a strong brew for use in ceremonies and tribal rituals. The colonists also used yaupon holly as a substitute for boxwood as described in the writings of Dr. Alexander Garden of Charleston: "It makes a very good and most beautiful hedge and may be kept as short and neat as the Box."

Yaupon holly develops an upright, oval form with multiple stems reaching a maximum height of 10 to 15 feet. Small textured, oval-shaped leaves grow from 1 to 1¹/₂ inches long. Tiny, inconspicuous white flowers develop in spring and are followed by shiny red, translucent berries in the fall.

Ideal for low- or medium-clipped hedges or for use in naturalistic plantings, it also can be limbed up to create an attractive multi-stem, small tree. Yaupon holly can be sheared to create topiary of various shapes and forms.

Growing in both sun and partial shade, it is perfectly at home in either wet or well-drained soils. An extremely tough and dependable plant, yaupon holly is free from insects and plant diseases. Once established, it will develop into an attractive, trouble-free plant.

Flowers and Ferns

Calendula (*Calendula officinalis*)

Calendula, or pot marigold, is a native of the Mediterranean area and has been grown in Europe since medieval times for use in flavoring foods. Apothecaries also used calendulas to make a soothing ointment for skin wounds and for treating various diseases and disorders. An old-fashioned garden annual grown in colonial gardens as early as 1650, new varieties today produce long-lasting single, double, and semi-double blossoms ranging in colors from creamy yellow to brilliant gold. Flowers of the calendula, which are produced during spring and fall,

grow to 4 inches in diameter on a single stem. Plants have a bushy habit of growth with dark green leaves that are aromatic and slightly sticky.

Ideal for mixed borders and beds, many new varieties have been developed within recent years with long flower stalks and fine colored blossoms that make them suitable for cutting. Calendulas also make excellent container plants for patios and window boxes. Calendulas grow best in a sunny or lightly shaded location in average soil that provides good drainage. Leaves of young plants are susceptible to mildew and are frequently eaten by slugs and snails. Several varieties that are frequently grown include *Pacific Beauty*, *Gypsy Festival*, and *Madarin*.

Common Geranium (*Pelargonium hortorum*)

Common geraniums, also called zonal or bedding geraniums, are complex hybrids whose parentage involves several species introduced into England from South Africa in the eighteenth and nineteenth centuries. Characterized by erect and somewhat succulent, branched stems with dark green, scalloped leaves, some varieties have foliage with zones of bronze to variegated markings in white, yellow, and cream. Individual flowers are borne in clusters on long, slender stems in colors ranging from red, pink, and salmon to white.

Although a perennial, the common geranium is generally treated as a tender annual. Geraniums typically are grown as bedding plants or, by tradition, used in window boxes, urns, hanging baskets, and other containers because of their ability to tolerate and prosper under hot, dry conditions. Long lasting in bloom, geraniums do well in full sun or in locations where there is only limited shade.

Geraniums perform best in fertile, well-drained soil and, because they are almost succulents, are very sensitive to over watering. For best results old plants should be discarded each fall and replaced with new ones the following spring.

Common Snapdragon (*Antirrhinum majus*)

The snapdragon, native to the Mediterranean region, derives its name from the Greek word *anti,* meaning like, and *rhinos,* or nose, referring to the snoutlike shape of the flowers. As a general rule snapdragons are usually treated as an annual and are discarded at the end of the first blooming season. Grown by generations of gardeners for their vertical accents of bright colors, many new horticultural varieties have been developed within recent years. Modern varieties include  a wide range of colors in hues of apricot, salmon, crimson, yellow, and white. Snapdragons are generally divided into three basic groups: tall, intermediate, and dwarf.

Snapdragons are one of the most rewarding of garden annuals, producing upright sturdy spikes of colorful flowers over a period of several months. They are extremely useful for flower beds where their neat, self-supporting habit makes them ideal for use in the back of a border. Excellent for cut flowers, the snapdragon can also be used effectively in window boxes or containers as accents when combined with other seasonal plants.

Snapdragons prefer a well-drained soil, a little on the alkaline side. They grow best in full sun but will also tolerate light shade. In Charleston and other areas with short mild winters, snapdragons will bloom in winter and early spring if set out in the fall.

Four-O'clock (*Mirabilis jalapa*)

A native of tropical America, the four-o'clock is a reliable herbaceous perennial that has been grown in old-world gardens since 1540, when it was imported to Europe from the Peruvian Andes. A favorite in Charleston gardens since colonial days, the four-o'clock is a rapid grower which within a single season can become large and shrublike. The four-o'clock is characterized by a broad spreading habit of growth. It produces long, tubular flowers that open in late afternoon, usually around four o'clock, from which it derives its common name. The four-o'clock was originally known as the Marvel of Peru because of its unique ability to produce different colored blossoms on a single plant. Flowers of the four-o'clock are usually 2 inches wide and range in color from red, yellow, and white to striped or blotched. Blossoms occur throughout the summer and well into the fall at a time when few other flowers are in bloom.

The four-o'clock is ideal for naturalistic plantings or for locations where it is difficult to get other plants to survive. While growing best in full sun, it will perform reasonably well in partial shade. The four-o'clock produces an abundance of seed and may escape from cultivation if left unchecked. While its foliage may be killed back to the ground in extremely cold winters, its large tuberous roots are seldom damaged and new foliage will appear the following spring. Disease and insect free, the four-o'clock is an extremely hardy and trouble-free plant that requires little care or attention and thrives with neglect.

Ginger Lily (*Hedychium coronarium*)

Grown for its tropical-like foliage and fragrant white flowers, ginger lily or butterfly lily, as it is sometimes called, is a vigorous, herbaceous perennial that is one of the great joys of Southern gardens. The bold, dark green leaves of this native Asian plant grow 3 to 4 feet high and from 8 to 10 inches across, forming large clumps of coarse-textured foliage. Clusters of large flowers resembling butterfly wings are produced on tall, erect spikes in late summer and fall when few other flowers are in bloom. The blossoms of the ginger lily produce a delicate fragrance reminiscent of gardenias.

Ideal for garden use in flower borders or for incorporation into foundation plantings, ginger lily is also interesting when grown in containers or tubs around terraces, patios, and pools. When used in pots, plants need ample root space and well-drained soil rich in organic material.

The ginger lily grows best in fertile soil and responds well to generous applications of fertilizer during the growing season and additional water during hot, dry periods. While tolerant of full sun, it prefers partial shade in locations with a northern orientation.

Generally free from pests and diseases, ginger lily is susceptible to frost and benefits from a protected location and a heavy mulch of leaves, pine straw, or other organic material. Periodic removal of old and damaged foliage is desirable to keep plants looking tidy and neat.

Holly Fern (*Cyrtomium falcatum*)

Holly fern is a coarse-textured, evergreen fern highly prized in gardens of the lower South. Its handsome, glossy, leathery leaves are borne on stiff, upright, arching fronds which grow to a height of 1 to 2 feet. The attractive, yellow-green spring growth of the holly fern creates a striking contrast to the dark green of older, mature foliage. The undersides of its leaves are light green and contain conspicuous brown spores that add an interesting touch to its overall appearance. Distinctive holly-like foliage also provides an interesting contrast with other plants and materials.

Suitable for patios, terraces, and courtyards, holly fern makes an excellent ground cover for shaded areas and can be naturalized effectively under tall trees and shrubs. It likes moist, well-drained soil that is high in organic matter. Growing both in partial and full shade, holly fern requires adequate moisture during hot summer months. Damaged winter foliage should be cut back before new spring growth begins. Mature plants should be separated and transplanted when crowded. Holly fern is excellent for small gardens as an accent plant or for use in shady spots along foundations, walls, walks, and paths.

Impatiens (*Impatiens wallerana*)

Impatiens, a native of Asia, are one of the South's most popular annuals for both sun and shade. Known by several common names including sultana, patient plant, and busy lizzie, this highly versatile plant provides a profusion of colorful blooms throughout the summer in shades of pink, salmon, red, purple, and white. Impatiens produce leaves that are dark green and glossy on soft juicy stems.

Impatiens can be obtained in an assortment of

sizes ranging in height from 12 inches (super elfins) to varieties that grow 2 feet tall. Ideal as a bedding plant, impatiens also do well in pots, hanging baskets, and window boxes. Within recent years, New Guinea hybrids with their vibrant flowers and variegated foliage have become popular additions to the garden. These striking and eye-catching plants are especially useful in pots for a shady patio or terrace.

Impatiens grow best in a moist, fertile soil. During hot summer months they require frequent watering and benefit from several inches of mulch to help conserve moisture. For best results impatiens should be fertilized at least once a month with an all-purpose liquid fertilizer.

Lantana (*Lantana camara*)

A native of the West Indies, lantana is a commonly grown perennial that has become natur-alized in many parts of the lower South. Before 1700 at least fifty varieties had been identified in the West Indies, some of which were used by the Spanish colonists for medical purposes. Introduced into Charleston quite early, no doubt by early settlers from Barbados, the lantana can be found growing today in many old gardens throughout the city.

The lantana is an extremely hardy and maintenance-free plant that develops a spreading or mounding habit of growth. Its stems and leaves are covered with short hairs and, when crushed, its leaves produce an unpleasant odor.

The lantana blooms profusely throughout summer and fall producing showy verbena-like flowers that range in color from yellow to orange, and change to red with age. Flowers are followed by black berries or drupes that are poisonous if eaten.

Tolerant of a wide range of growing conditions, the lantana does best in poor, well-drained soil in a sunny location. It is not especially cold hardy, and new foliage may be damaged during extremely cold winters. It should be pruned back in the fall for best results the following spring. Ideal as a specimen plant or in a flower border, lantana is also useful when grown in pots or tubs.

Larkspur (*Delphinium consolida*)

A native of southern Europe and naturalized in many parts of North America, larkspur or annual delphinium is a traditional favorite in old gardens of the South. The common name, larkspur, is derived from a single backward pointing spur on each flower that resembles the spur of a lark's foot. A true annual, larkspur is prized for its finely cut, threadlike leaves and clusters of white, blue, purple, and pink flowers which bloom in late spring and early summer.

A graceful and decorative addition to any garden, larkspur generally reaches 2 to 3 feet in height making it an excellent choice as a background plant in beds and borders. The tall spikelike flower clusters of larkspur are excellent for cutting. Like many annuals, larkspur has a rather short blooming season, rapidly fading with the onset of summer heat. For this reason seeds should be sown in autumn or winter to insure early germination in spring. To encourage reseeding, plants should be allowed to remain in place until seed pods have fully matured. Larkspur needs full sun and a rich, well-drained soil

for best results. New seedlings should be fertilized soon after germination with a complete garden fertilizer or well-rotted manure.

Morning Flower (*Ruellia brittoniana*)

Native to Mexico, *Ruellia brittoniana* has become naturalized in the deep south, particularly in Florida and several of the Gulf Coast states. The genus *Ruellia* was named for Jean de la Ruelle (1474–1537), an early French physician and botanist. *Ruellia* is known in Charleston as the Morning or Breakfast Flower because its flowers open in the morning and close by early afternoon.

Generally described as an herbaceous perennial, *Ruellia* is an extremely hardy and tenacious plant that will grow in difficult locations and survive under adverse conditions. Mature plants reach a height of 3 feet and produce elongated, willow-like leaves that are purplish in color. Leaves usually grow to be 12 inches long and $3/4$ inches wide. The flowers are 1 to $1^1/_2$ inches long and are lavender-blue to blue-violet in color. Blooms occur continuously from May to September followed by long bean-like pods with seed that germinate quite easily.

Ruellia makes an excellent plant for hot, sunny locations, particularly along the base of a fence or garden wall. It is also useful as an accent plant for a perennial border. At the end of the season, plants should be pruned to the ground and lightly mulched. *Ruellia* is a reliable and trouble-free plant that is resistant to both disease and insects.

Pansy (*Viola tricolor* var. *hortensis*)

Pansies, as known today, are relatively recent introductions resulting from crosses between older species, including johnny-jump-up (*Viola tricolor*) which is an ancestral parent of modern day varieties. Except for distinctive flower markings resembling human facial characteristics, it is difficult to associate the large splendid blooms of modern hybrids with the diminutive flowers of their early ancestors. Ranging in size from 2 to 4 inches, modern varieties produce flowers that include a wide range of colors and combinations including white, cream, yellow, orange, pink, purple, blue, and maroon.

Pansies are extremely popular for beds and borders whether planted by themselves or as companion plants with hyacinths, tulips, daffodils, and other spring-flowering bulbs. They are also ideally suited for window boxes, pots, urns, or containers where their low dense habit of growth and colorful flowers provide a constant source of pleasure throughout late winter and spring.

Typically grown as an annual in the South, pansies prefer a moderately fertile, well-drained soil and grow best in full sun or light shade. In Charleston and other areas with mild winters, pansies are planted in November and produce a fine display of flowers during winter and spring, but rapidly fade with the onset of heat in late May and June.

Plumbago (*Plumbago auriculata*)

A native South African plant, plumbago is a shrubby perennial grown extensively throughout the lower South for its profusion of bright blue flowers that occur from May to November. Growing to a height of 2 to 3 feet, plumbago develops into a sprawling, semi-climbing shrub that becomes vine-like if allowed to grow unpruned.  Its leaves occur along the length of the stem and are fine-textured and light green in color. Its azure blue, phlox-like flowers develop in large, rounded clusters about $1\frac{1}{2}$ inches long and approximately 1 inch across.

Useful for training against walls, columns, and fences (or as an informal hedge or bedding plant), plumbago can also be grown in containers for use around patios, terraces, or pools. Its rambling habit of growth creates interesting visual effects when allowed to cascade over the side of pots, tubs, and planters.

For best results, plumbago should be grown in full sun, in well-drained, reasonably fertile soil. A southern or southeastern location is particularly desirable. Several applications of fertilizer during the growing season are recommended. Plants should be pruned heavily in late winter and early spring. Plumbago is susceptible to red spider and occasional infestations of mealy bugs.

Shrimp Plant (*Justicia brandegeana*)

Native to Mexico, the shrimp plant is frequently grown in gardens of the lower South as an outdoor ornamental and in the north as an indoor or a greenhouse plant. The genus, *Justicia*, commemorates James Justice, a Scottish gardener who died in 1754.

The shrimp plant is a loosely branched and medium textured sub-shrub, growing 1 to 3 feet tall, that develops a broad, irregular form with rather weak stems and long hairy leaves. This unusual and somewhat curious plant produces showy, orange-red to reddish-brown flowers (bracts) that have the distinct shape and appearance of a shrimp, from which it derives its common name. Flowers are borne in great profusion throughout summer and fall. As the shrimp plant begins blooming at an early age, flowers should be removed when small to encourage well-developed and bushy plants.

Attractive additions to outdoor beds, borders, and other ornamental plantings, the shrimp plant is also useful for pots or containers on a patio or terrace where its blossoms add a colorful and unique touch to a landscape setting. For best results plants should be grown in a porous, well-drained soil that receives several hours of direct sunlight, ideally during the early hours of the day.

The shrimp plant requires winter protection and, even when grown in sheltered locations, is often killed back to the ground during cold winters. Plants should be pruned annually in order to maintain an attractive shape as older specimens become straggly and unsightly with age. Free from most pests and diseases, mature plants benefit from regular applications of liquid fertilizer from spring through fall.

Southern Maidenhair Fern (*Adiantum capillus-veneris*)

A native of subtropical and warm-temperate regions of the world, including the southern United States, southern maidenhair fern is generally considered one of the most popular and beautiful of the

southern ferns. Admired for its delicate, soft green foliage, it is grown outside in the South and is used indoors as a container plant in the North. The leaves of southern maidenhair fern were used for their medicinal qualities by early herbalists in many tonics, extracts, syrups, and tinctures.

Southern maidenhair fern is an herbaceous perennial characterized by thin, fan-shaped leaflets that comprise lacy, fine-textured fronds and dark bronze stems. It is often used in Charleston gardens as a ground cover along shady walks and patios or as an accent plant in enclosed courtyards, walled gardens, or protected patios and terraces. Its ability to tolerate dense shade, high moisture, and humidity make it ideal for difficult locations where few other plants will grow.

For best results southern maidenhair fern should be planted in a location that affords protection from midday sun and drying winds. It also requires a well-drained, moist soil high in organic material and nutrients. A slow release fertilizer is recommended. As foliage is usually killed in winter, plants should be cut back after the first frost and lightly mulched during winter.

Stock (*Matthiola incana*)

Common stock, native to southern Europe, was extremely popular during the sixteenth and seventh centuries and probably long before. The genus,

Matthiola, was named in honor of Pierandrer Mattioli, an Italian physician and botanist who lived in the sixteenth century. A longtime favorite in American gardens, stock was called gilliflower during

George Washington's day.

Stock is a hardy annual grown for its ruffled flowers that range in color from pink, rose, and purple to yellow and white. Both single and double flowering varieties are available. Stock is excellent for beds and borders and is also prized as cut flowers because of its showy and fragrant flowers which produce a penetrating, spicy perfume. Stock does well in containers, and the dwarf bedding varieties are ideal as additions to window boxes when combined with other winter and spring blooming plants.

It grows best in a sunny location in light, fertile soil that provides good drainage. In Charleston and other areas with short, mild winters, stock should be planted in fall or early spring for blossoms that will last into early summer before temperatures become too warm. After being transplanted stock should receive a weekly application of a diluted liquid fertilizer to insure healthy and well-developed plants.

HISTORIC PLANTS FOR PERIOD GARDENS

The gardens of Charleston and the Carolina Lowcountry were similar in plan and in the use of flowers and ornamental shrubs including such favorites as camellias (*Camellia japonica*), tea olive (*Osmanthus fragrans*), laurustinus (*Viburnum tinus*), oleander (*Nerium oleander*), pomegranate (*Punica granatum*), crape myrtle (*Lagerstroemia indica*), spice tree (*Laurus noblis*), gardenia (*Gardenia jasminoides*), acacia (*Acacia farnesiana*), and many old-fashioned bulbs. Box (*Buxus sempervirens*), cassena holly (*Ilex cassine*), cherry laurel (*Prunus caroliniana*), and yaupon (*Ilex vomitoria*) were commonly used either for clipped hedges or skillfully fashioned into topiary of fanciful shapes.

Roses were also grown in old Charleston gardens from the earliest of times. For centuries the Cherokee rose, with its large white flowers and glossy evergreen leaves, has festooned many a Charleston garden wall. Old garden favorites include the Cinnamon, the York and Lancaster, the Musk, and the Damask. These in time were followed by Safrano, Duke of Luxemborg, Devoniensis, Paul Neyron, Reine Marie Henriette, Duchesse de Brabant, and Madame Plantier. Charleston's own contribution to the heritage of roses includes Champneys' Pink Cluster, Isabella Gray, and Fraser's Pink Musk, the latter being developed around 1818 by John Fraser.

A valuable source of information on historic plants for period gardens was prepared in the 1930s by Emma Richardson, assistant to the director of the Charleston Museum. Richardson was assigned the task of re-creating a period garden for the

Hollyhock
(*Althaea rosea*)

Roses have been grown in Charleston gardens since the earliest of times.

Heyward-Washington House in which President Washington resided while visiting Charleston in 1791. As no vestige of the original garden remained, it was decided that a re-created design typifying a late eighteenth-century Charleston garden should be developed and that only plants introduced into cultivation prior to that date should be used. Relying on *Loudon's Encyclopedia of Plants* (1841 edition), Richardson developed a detailed list of plants appropriate for use in a garden of that period. While the dates referenced in Richardson's list indicate the approximate year each plant was introduced into England, it can be safely assumed that because of Charleston's close ties with that country, these plants arrived in the colony shortly thereafter. Emma Richardson's research was published in *The Charleston Museum Leaflet No. 15,* as "The Heyward Washington House Garden." With permission of the museum the list is presented in its entirety as a valuable source of information for use in restoring and re-creating period gardens.

HISTORIC PLANT LIST

From *The Charleston Museum Leaflet No. 15* prepared by Emma Richardson.
Courtesy of The Charleston Museum, Charleston, South Carolina.

Common Name	Scientific Name	Native Country	Year of Introduction
Aconite: Monkshood	*Aconitum napellus*	Europe	1596
African Lily	*Agapanthus umbellatus*	Cape of Good Hope	1692
Ageratum:	*Ageratum conyzoides*	America	1714
Hardy	*A. coelestinum*	North America	1732
Atamasco Lily	*Zephyranthes atamasco*	North America	1629
Althea	*Hibiscus syriacus*	Syria	1596
Alyssum: Golden Tuft	*Alyssum saxatile*	Candia	1710
Sweet	*A. maritimum*	Britain *	
Arabis: Rock Cress	*Arabis alpina*	Switzerland	1596
Aster: Stokes'	*Stokesia cyanea*	Carolina	1766
Autumn Crocus	*Colchicum autumnale*	Britain	
Baby's Breath:	*Gypsophila paniculata*	Siberia	1759
Creeping	*G. repens*	Siberia	1774
Balsam: Lady's Slipper	*Impatiens balsamina*	East Indies	1596
Banana Shrub	*Magnolia (Michelia) fuscata*	China	1789

*Plants marked as "Britain" are British wildflowers that have long been cultivated.

Common Name	Scientific Name	Native Country	Year of Introduction
Bee Balm	*Monarda didyma*	North America	1752
Bellflower: Great-flowered	*Platycodon grandiflorum*	Siberia	1782
Bignonia: Yellow	*Bignonia unguis*	West Indies	1757
Box	*Buxus sempervirens*	Britain	
Calendula	*Calendula officinalis*	Southern Europe	1573
Camellia	*Camellia japonica*	China	1739
Campanula:			
Bluebells of Scotland	*Campanula rotundifolia*	Britain	
Canterbury Bells	*C. medium*	Germany	1597
Carpathian Harebell	*C. carpatica*	Carpathian Alps	1774
Clustered	*C. glomerata*	Britain	
Creeping	*C. rapunculoides*	Britain	
Steeple	*C. pyramidalis*	Carniola	1696
Campion:			
Double-flowered Scarlet	*Lychnis viscaria flore pleno*	Britain	
Lychnis	*L. chalcedonica*	Russia	1596
Candytuft: Annual	*Iberis umbellata*	Southern Europe	1596
Perennial	*I. sempervirens*	Sicily	1679
Canna	*Canna indica*	India	1570
Chrysanthemum: Annual	*Chrysanthemum coronarium*	Sicily	1692
Citrina: Lemon Verbena	*Lippia citriodora*	Chile	1784
Cockscomb	*Celosia cristata*	Asia	1570
Columbine:	*Aquilegia vulgaris*	Britain	
Canadian	*A. canadensis*	North America	1640

Common Name	Scientific Name	Native Country	Year of Introduction
Convolvulus: Three-colored	*Convolvulus tricolor*	Southern Europe	1629
Coralberry: India Currant	*Symphoricarpus orbiculatus (vulgaris)*	North America	1730
Coreopsis: Tickseed	*Coreopsis lanceolata*	Carolina	1724
Cornflower: Ragged Robin	*Centaurea cyanus*	Britain	
Crepe Myrtle	*Lagerstroemia indica*	East Indies	1759
Cupid's Dart	*Catananche caerulea*	Southern Europe	1596
Cypress Vine	*Ipomoea quamoclit*	East Indies	1629
Daisy: English	*Bellis perennis*	Britain	
Ox-eye	*Chrysanthemum leucanthemum*	Britain	
Dragonhead: False	*Physostegia virginiana*	America	1683
Great-flowered	*P. grandiflora*	Siberia	1759
Elephant's Ear	*Caladium esculentum*	America	1739
Four-o'clock	*Mirabilis jalapa*	West Indies	1596
Foxglove	*Digitalis purpurea*	Britain	
Fragrant Olive: Tea Olive	*Osmanthus fragrans*	China	1771
Fringe Tree	*Chionanthus virginica*	North America	1736
Fritillaria:	*Fritillaria meleagris*	Britain	
Crown Imperial	*F. imperialis*	Persia	1596
Gardenia	*Gardenia floridana*	China	1754
Giant Spider	*Cleome gigantea*	South America	1774
Globe Amaranth	*Gomphrena globosa*	India	1714
Grape Hyacinth	*Muscari botryoides*	Italy	1596

Common Name	Scientific Name	Native Country	Year of Introduction
Guernsey Lily	*Nerine sarniensis*	Japan	1659
Heart's Ease: Johnny-jump-up	*Viola tricolor*	Britain	
Heliotrope	*Heliotropum peruvianum*	Peru	1757
Hen-and-Chickens: Houseleek	*Sempervivum globiferum*	Germany	1731
Hollyhock	*Althea rosea*	China	1573
Honeysuckle: Coral	*Lonicera sempervirens*	North America	1656
Hyacinth: Dutch	*Hyacinth orientalis*	Levant	1596
Roman	*H. orientalis* var. *albulus*	Levant	1596
Hydrangea	*Hydrangea opuloides*	China	1788
Iris: Crested	*Iris cristata*	North America	1754
Dwarf	*I. pumila*	Austria	1596
German	*I. germanica*	Germany	1573
Siberian	*I. siberica*	Siberia	1596
Spanish	*I. hispanica*	Spain	1653
Sulphur-colored	*I. ochroleuca*	Levant	1757
Various-colored	*I. versicolor*	North America	1732
Ivy: Kenilworth	*Linaria cymbalaria*	Britain	
Ixia	*Ixia crateroides*	Cape of Good Hope	1778
Japanese Plum:			
Medlar: Loquat	*Eriobotrya japonica*	Japan	1787
Lantana	*Lantana camara*	West Indies	1691
Larkspur: Annual	*Delphinium ajacis*	Switzerland	1573
Single and Double	*D. grandiflorum*	Siberia	1741
Laurustinus	*Viburnum tinus*	Southern Europe	1596

Common Name	Scientific Name	Native Country	Year of Introduction
Lavender Cotton	*Santolina chamaecyparissus*	Southern Europe	1573
Lavender: Sweet	*Lavendula vera*	Southern Europe	1568
Lily: Copper-colored	*Hemerocallis fulva*	Levant	1596
Lemon	*H. flava*	Siberia	1596
Madonna	*Lillium candidum*	Levant	1596
Scarlet Turk's Cap	*L. chalcedonicum*	Levant	1596
Turk's Cap	*L. martagon*	Germany	1659
Lobelia: Cardinal-flower	*Lobelia cardinalis*	Virginia	1629
Great-blue	*L. syphilitica*	Virginia	1665
Locust: Pink	*Robinia hispida*	Carolina	1743
Love-in-a-puff: Balloon Vine	*Cardiospermum halicacabum*	India	1594
Marigold: African	*Tagetes erecta*	Mexico	1596
French	*T. patula*	Mexico	1573
Mignonette	*Reseda odorata*	Egypt	1752
Milfoil: Yarrow: Dwarf	*Achillea tomentosa*	Britain	
White	*A. millefolium*	Britain	
Mimosa	*Albizzia julibrissin*	Levant	1745
Moneywort	*Lysimachia nummularia*	Britain	
Morning Glory: Ivy-leaved	*Ipomoea hederacea*	North America	1729
Moss Pink	*Phlox subulata*	North America	1786
Narcissus: Butter and Eggs	*Narcissus incomparabilis*	Portugal	1629
Daffodil	*N. bicolor*	Spain	1629
Jonquil	*N. jonquilla*	Spain	1596
Many-flowered	*N. orientalis*	Levant	

Common Name	Scientific Name	Native Country	Year of Introduction
Paper-white	*N. papyraceus*		*Ancient times*
Poet's	*N. poeticus*	Southern Europe	
Rush-leaved	*N. triandrus*	Portugal	1629
Small	*N. minor*	Spain	1629
Trumpet	*N. major*	Spain	1629
Nasturtium: Dwarf	*Tropaeolum minus*	Peru	1596
Tall	*T. majus*	Peru	1686
Oleander	*Nerium oleander*	Southern Europe	1596
Oxalis: Yellow	*Oxalis caprina*	Cape of Good Hope	1757
Parkinsonia	*Parkinsonia aculeata*	West Indies	1739
Pea: Perennial	*Lathyrus latifolius*	Britain	
Sweet	*L. odoratus*	Sicily	1700
Periwinkle: Larger	*Vinca major*	Britain	
Trailing	*V. minor*	Britain	
Pink: Cheddar	*Dianthus caesius*	Britain	
Chinese	*D. chinensis*	China	1713
Clove	*D. plumarius*	Europe	1629
Gillyflower	*D. caryophyllus*	Britain	
Maiden	*D. deltoides*	Britain	
Sand-loving	*D. arenarius*	Europe	
Sweet William	*D. barbatus*	Germany	1573
Poinciana: Royal	*Poinciana pulcherrima*	East Indies	1691
Pomegranate	*Punica granatum*	Southern Europe	1548

Common Name	Scientific Name	Native Country	Year of Introduction
Popinac	*Acacia farnesiana*	Santo Domingo	1656
Poppy: Corn	*Papaver rhoeas*	Britain	
Iceland	*P. nudicaule*	Siberia	1730
Oriental	*P. orientalis*	Levant	1714
Portulaca	*Portulaca sativa*	South America	1652
Ranunculus	*Ranunculus asiaticus*	Levant	1596
Red Bud: Judas Tree	*Cercis siliquastum*	Southern Europe	1596
Red-hot Poker	*Tritoma uvaria*	Cape of Good Hope	1707
Rose: Ayrshire	*Rosa arvensis*		*Cultivated since* 1750
Cabbage	*R. centrifolia*	Southern Europe	1596
Cherokee	*R. laevigata*	China	1780
Damask	*R. damascena*	Levant	1573
Dog	*R. canina*	Britain	
French	*R. gallica*	Southern Europe	1596
Musk	*R. moschata*	Barbary	1596
Pink Moss	*R. muscosa (communis)*	Holland	*ca.* 1596
Red Provence	*R. centriolia* var.	Southern Europe	1596
Scotch	*R. spinossissima*	Britain	
Shining-leaved	*R. lucida*	North America	1724
Sweetbrier	*R. rubiginosa*	Britain	
Wild Rose	*R. carolina*	North America	1726
York	*R. alba*	Crimea	1597
York and Lancaster	*R. damascena* var.	Levant	1573

Common Name	Scientific Name	Native Country	Year of Introduction
Rose of Sharon	*Hibiscus rosa-sinensis*	East Indies	1731
Rudbeckia:	*Rudbeckia purpurea*	North America	1699
Black-eyed Susan	*R. hirta*	North America	1714
Scarlet Ipomoea	*Ipomoea coccinea*	West Indies	1713
Sedum: Golden Moss	*Sedum acre*	Britain	
Rose	*S. dasyphyllum*	Britain	
Tall	*S. altissimum*	Southern Europe	1769
Snapdragon	*Antirrhinum majus*	Britain	
Snowball	*Viburnum opulus sterile*	Britain	
Snow Drop	*Galanthus nivalis*	Britain	
Snow Flake	*Leucojum vernum*	Germany	1596
(locally known as Snow Drop)			
Snow-on-the-Mountain	*Euphorbia emarginata*	Italy	1758
Speedwell:	*Veronica longifolia*	Southern Europe	1731
Hoary	*V. incana*	Russia	1759
Spikenard: Chaste Tree	*Vitex Agnus-castus*	Sicily	1570
Squills: English Blue Bells	*Scilla nutans*	Britain	
Two-leaved	*S. bifolia*	Britain	
Spanish	*S. campanulata*	Spain	1633
Star-of-Bethlehem	*Ornithogalum arabicum*	Egypt	1629
Stock: Gillyflower	*Mathiola incana*	Britain	
Ten-weeks	*M. annua* var.	Southern Europe	1731
Strawberry Geranium	*Saxifraga sarmentosa*	China	1771
Strawberry Shrub	*Calycanthus floridus*	Carolina	1726

Common Name	Scientific Name	Native Country	Year of Introduction
Sunflower:	*Helianthus annuus*	South America	1596
Double	*H. multiflorus*	North America	1597
Sweet Rocket	*Hesperis matronalis*	Italy	1597
Syringa: Lemon	*Philadelphus coronarius*	Southern Europe	1596
Large-flowered	*P. grandiflorus*	Carolina native	
Talinum: Creeping	*Talinum patens*	South America	1776
Thrift	*Armeria maritima*	Britain	
Tuberose: Single and Double	*Polianthes tuberosa*	East Indies	1629
Tulip: Clusius's	*Tulipa clusiana*	Sicily	1636
Common	*T. gesneriana*	Levant	1577
Wild	*T. sylvestris*	Britain	
Valerian	*Valeriana officinalis*	Britain	
Vinca	*Vinca rosea* and *alba*	East Indies	1756
Violet	*Viola odorata*	Britain	
Wall Flower	*Cheiranthus cheiri*	Southern Europe	1573
Wintersweet	*Meratia praecox*	China	1766

Bibliography

Adams, Marty Whaley. "My Mother's Garden." *Southern Accents*, July–August 1989, 94–103.

Alleyne, Warren, and Henry Fraser. *The Barbados-Carolina Connection*. Hong Kong: Macmillan, 1988.

Ash, Thomas. *Carolina, or a Description of the Present State of that Country*. London, 1682.

Audubon, John James. *The Birds of America*. New York: Macmillan, 1941.

———. *Ornithological Biography*. Vol 2. Edinburgh: Adam Black, 1834.

Bartram, William. *Travels Through North and South Carolina, Georgia, East and West Florida*. New York: Macy-Masius, 1933.

Berkeley, Edmund, and Dorothy Smith. *Dr. Alexander Garden of Charles Town*. Chapel Hill: University of North Carolina Press, 1969.

Briggs, Loutrel W. *Charleston Gardens*. Columbia: University of South Carolina Press, 1951.

———. "Charleston's Famous Gardens." *House and Garden*, March 1939, 45, 94–95.

Bryant, William Cullen, ed. *Picturesque America*. Vol. 1. New York: D. Appleton and Company, 1874.

Catesby, Mark. *The Natural History of Carolina, Florida, and the Bahama Islands*. 2 vols. London, 1731–1743.

Coker, William Chambers. "The Garden of André Michaux." *Journal of Elisha Mitchell Scientific Society* 27 (1911): 65–72.

Cran, Marion. *Gardens of America*. New York: Macmillan, 1932.

Darlington, William, ed. *Memorials of John Bartram and Humphry Marshall*. Philadelphia, 1849.

Dezallier d'Argenville, A. J. *The Theory and Practice of Gardening*. Translated from the French original by John James. London: Geo. James, 1712.

Downing, Andrew Jackson. *Treatise on the Theory and Practice of Landscape Gardening*. New York: Wiley and Putnam, 1841.

Drayton, John. "The Carolinian Florist." Manuscript in the Charleston Library Society, Charleston, S.C.

Duncan, Frances. "Charleston Gardens." *The Century Magazine*, March 1907, 705–19.

Dunn, Richard S. *Sugar and Slaves: The Rise of the Planter Class in the English West Indies, 1624–1713*. New York: Norton, 1972.

Elliot, Stephen. *Sketch of the Botany of South Carolina and Georgia*. 2 vols. Charleston: J. R. Schenk, 1821–1824.

Feduccia, Alan. *Catesby's Birds of Colonial America*. Chapel Hill: University of North Carolina Press, 1985.

Fitzpatrick, John C., ed. *The Diaries of George Washington 1748–1799*. Vol. 4. Cambridge: The Riverside Press, 1925.

Fraser, Charles. *Reminiscences of Charleston.* Charleston: John Russell, 1854.

Hall, Lieutenant Francis. *Travels in Canada and the United States in 1816 and 1817.* London: Hurst, Rees, Orme and Brown, 1819.

Hawthorne, Hildegarde. *The Lure of the Garden.* New York: The Century Company, 1911.

Hedrick, U. P. *A History of Horticulture in America to 1860*. Portland: Timber Press, 1950.

Heyward, DuBose. "Charleston: Where Mellow Past and Present Meet." *National Geographic* 75, no. 3 (March 1939): 273–312.

Hume, Harold Hardrada. *Gardening in the Lower South.* New York: Macmillan, 1929.

Hunt, Peter, ed. *The Book of Garden Ornament.* London: J. M. Dent, 1974.

Jones, Katharine M. *The Plantation South.* Indianapolis: Boggs-Merrill, 1984.

Lane, Mills. *Architecture of the Old South: South Carolina.* Savannah: Beehive Press, 1989.

Leighton, Ann. *America Gardens of the Nineteenth Century.* Amherst: University of Massachusetts Press, 1987.

Linley, John. "Architecture, Landscape Architecture, City Planning: Charleston and Savannah." In *Georgia Landscape,* 7–8. Athens: School of Environmental Design, 1992.

———. *The Georgia Catalog: Historic American Buildings Survey.* Athens: University of Georgia, 1982.

Lockwood, Alice B., comp. & ed. *Gardens of Colony and State.* 2 vols. New York: Charles Scribner's Sons, 1931–1934.

Marion, John Francis. *The Charleston Story: Scenes from a City's History.* Harrisburg: Stackpole Books, 1978.

McAden, Ann, and Boyd Saunders. *Alfred Hutty and the Charleston Renaissance.* Orangeburg, S.C.: Sandlapper Publishing, 1990.

McCrady, Edward. *History of South Carolina Under the Royal Government.* New York: Macmillan, 1897.

Meriwether, Margaret Babcock, ed. *The Carolinian Florist of Governor John Drayton of South Carolina, 1766–1822.* Columbia: South Caroliniana Library of the University of South Carolina, 1943.

Michaux, André. *Flora Boreali—Americana.* Paris, 1803.

Michaux, F. A. *Travels to the West of the Alleghany Mountains in the States of Ohio, Kentucky and Tennesea, and Back to Charleston by the Upper Carolines.* 3d English ed. London: B. Crosby and J. F. Hughes, 1805.

Molloy, Robert. *Charleston, A Gracious Heritage.* New York: D. Appleton-Century Company, 1947.

Noble, Allen G. *Houses.* Vol. 1 of *Wood, Brick, and Stone: The North American Settlement Landscape.* Amherst: University of Massachusetts Press, 1984.

Odenwald, Neil G., and James R. Turner. *Identification Selection and Use of Southern Plants for Landscape Design.* Baton Rouge: Claitor's Press, 1987.

Olmsted, John Charles. "Charleston, South Carolina Trip Report—September 21, 1910." Olmsted Papers, Manuscript Division, Library of Congress.

Pinckney, Elise. "Still Mindful of the English Way: 250 Years of Middleton Place on the Ashley." *South Carolina Historical Magazine* 92, no. 3 (July 1991): 149–71.

———. *Thomas and Elizabeth Lamboll: Early Charleston Gardeners*. Charleston: Charleston Museum Publishing, 1969.

Porcher, Dr. Francis Peyre. *Resources of the Southern Fields and Forests*. Charleston: Evans and Cogswell, 1863.

Ramsay, David. *The History of South Carolina, from its First Settlement in 1670 to the Year 1809*. Charleston: David Longworth, 1809.

Ravenel, Harriott Horry (Rutledge). "Mrs. St. Julien Ravenel." In *Charleston, the Place and the People*. New York: Macmillan, 1906.

———. "Mrs. St. Julien Ravenel." In *Eliza Lucas Pinckney*. New York: Charles Scribner's Sons, 1896.

Richardson, Emma B. "Charleston Garden Plats." *The Charleston Museum Leaflet No. 19*. Charleston: The Charleston Museum, 1943.

———. "The Heyward-Washington House Garden." *The Charleston Museum Leaflet No. 15*. Charleston, The Charleston Museum, 1941.

Rogers, George C., Jr. *Charleston in the Age of the Pinckneys*. Columbia: University of South Carolina Press, 1980.

Rosen, Robert N. *A Short History of Charleston*. San Francisco: Lexikos, 1982.

Sarudy, Barbara Wells. "South Carolina Seed Merchants and Nurserymen Before 1820." *Magnolia, Bulletin of the Southern Garden History Society*, Winter 1992, 6–10.

Severens, Kenneth. *Charleston—Antebellum Architecture and Civic Destiny*. Knoxville: University of Tennessee Press, 1988.

Severens, Martha R., and Charles L. Wyrick, Jr. *Charles Fraser of Charleston Essay on the Man, His Art, and His Times*. Charleston: Carolina Art Association, 1983.

Shaffer, Edward Terry Hendrie. *Carolina Gardens*. Chapel Hill: University of North Carolina Press, 1939.

Simons, Albert, and S. Lapham, Jr., eds. *Charleston South Carolina*. Vol. 1 of *The Octagon Library of Early American Architecture*. New York: Press of the American Institute of Architects, 1927.

Smith, Alice Ravenel Huger, and D. E. Smith. *The Dwelling Houses of Charleston, South Carolina*. Philadelphia: J. B. Lippincott, 1917.

Squibb, Robert. *The Gardener's Calender for South-Carolina, Georgia, and North-Carolina*. Athens: University of Georgia Press, 1980.

Stoney, Samuel Gaillard. "Art Gallery Today Opens Exhibit Marking 200th Anniversary of Beauty Spot." *Charleston News and Courier*, 24 March 1941.

———. *Charleston: Azaleas and Old Bricks*. Boston: Houghton Mifflin, 1937.

———. *Plantations of the Carolina Low Country*. Albert Simons and Samuel Lapham, Jr., eds. Charleston: Carolina Art Association, 1938.

———. *This is Charleston: An Architectural Survey of a Unique American City*. Charleston: Carolina Art Association, 1990.

Taylor, Raymond L. *Plants of Colonial Days: A Guide to 160 Flowers, Shrubs, and Trees in the Gardens of Colonial Williamsburg*. Williamsburg: Colonial Williamsburg, 1952.

Very, Rosemary. "The Walled Gardens of Charleston." *Horticulture*, April 1988, 41–48.

Walter, Thomas. *Flora Caroliniana*. London: J. Fraser, 1788.

Wedda, John. *Gardens of the American South*. New York: Galahad Books, 1971.

Wigginton, Brooks E. *Trees and Shrubs for the Southern Coastal Plain*. Athens: University of Georgia Press, 1957.

Index

Illustration Credits

Page i. Detail of a photograph by the author.

Page ii. *A Garden in Charleston,* from *Picturesque America,* 1874.

Pages vi, viii, ix, x, xi. Photographs by the author.

Pages vi, xii. Photographs by Alexander Wallace. Copyright 1991 Alexander L. Wallace.

Page 3. Illustration from *The Natural History of Carolina, Florida, and the Bahama Islands* by Mark Catesby. Courtesy of the Charleston Library Society, Charleston, S.C.

Page 4. Courtesy of Dumbarton Oaks, Studies in Landscape Architecture, photo archive.

Page 5. Illustration from *The Natural History of Carolina, Florida, and the Bahama Islands* by Mark Catesby. Courtesy of Colonial Williamsburg Foundation.

Page 7. Illustration from *Choix de plus belles fleurs* (1829) by P. J. Redouté. Courtesy of Hunt Institute for Botanical Documentation, Carnegie Mellon University, Pittsburgh, Penn.

Page 8. Courtesy of Hunt Institute for Botanical Documentation, Carnegie Mellon University, Pittsburgh, Penn.

Page 10. Illustration from John James Audubon's *The Birds of America.* Special Collections Department, Robert Scott Small Library, College of Charleston (S.C.).

Page 11. Illustration from *Les roses* (1817–24) by P. J. Redouté. Courtesy of Hunt Institute for Botanical Documentation, Carnegie Mellon University, Pittsburgh, Penn.

Page 12. Courtesy of Hunt Institute for Botanical Documentation, Carnegie Mellon University, Pittsburgh, Penn.

Page 13. Photograph by the author.

Page 15. Illustration from John James Audubon's *The Birds of America.* Special Collections Department, Robert Scott Small Library, College of Charleston (S.C.).

Page 16. Illustration from A. J. Dezallier d'Argenville's *The Theory and Practice of Gardening;* reprinted in *Gardens of Colony and State,* vol. 2. Courtesy of the Garden Club of America.

Page 19. *A View near Charleston, 1801* by Charles Fraser. Courtesy of Gibbes Museum of Art/ Carolina Art Association.

Page 20. *Charleston From the Bay* from *Picturesque America* (1874). Courtesy of the Charleston Museum, Charleston, S.C.

Page 21. Photograph from Library of Congress collection.

Page 23. Map showing certain plantations in the

lower part of South Carolina. Courtesy of the Carolina Art Association and Dover Publications, Inc.

Pages 24–25. Plan based on drawings by A. T. S. Stoney and Garrow and Associates, Inc.

Page 26. Courtesy of Middleton Place Foundation.

Page 27. Plan of Middleton Place by A. T. S. Stoney. Courtesy of Gibbes Museum of Art/ Carolina Art Association and Dover Publications.

Pages 28, 29, 30, 31. Photographs by Derek Fell.

Page 32. Plan courtesy of the Charleston Museum, Charleston, S.C.

Page 34. Plan based on drawing contained in *Gardens of Colony and State,* vol 2. Courtesy of the Garden Club of America.

Page 35. Photograph courtesy of Smithsonian Institution, Archives of American Gardens, Garden Club of America Collection.

Pages 36–37. Copyright 1988 Southern Living, Inc. Reprinted with permission.

Page 38 (left). Photograph by the author.

Page 38 (right). Photograph from Library of Congress collection.

Pages 39 and 40. Photographs from *The Century Magazine.* Courtesy of the Charleston Library Society, Charleston, S.C.

Page 41. Photograph by Derek Fell.

Page 43. Courtesy of *Post and Courier,* Charleston, S.C.

Page 45. Illustration from *Woman's Home Companion* May 1926, courtesy of the Charleston Library Society, Charleston, S.C. Originally published by Crowell/Collier Publishers, purchased by McMillan Press.

Page 47. Copyright 1990 Southern Living, Inc. Reprinted with permission.

Page 48. Photograph by Alexander Wallace. Copyright 1991 Alexander L. Wallace.

Page 49 (top). Photograph courtesy of Mary Palmer Dargan.

Page 49 (bottom). Illustration from *Charleston Gardens.* Reprinted with permission of Janet Tantum and courtesy of House & Garden, copyright 1939 (renewed 1967) by Condé Nast Publications Inc.

Pages 50, 51 (top). Photographs by the author.

Page 51 (bottom). Photograph by Paul Barton.

Page 52. Plans by the author.

Page 53. Georgia Historical Society, GHS Archives.

Page 55. *The Reserve in Summer* by Alice Ravenel Huger Smith. Courtesy of Gibbes Museum of Art/Carolina Art Association.

Page 57 (top). Photograph by Derek Fell.

Page 57 (bottom). Photograph by Terry Richardson.

Page 58. Illustration from *Charleston Gardens.* Reprinted with permission of Janet Tantum and courtesy of House & Garden, copyright 1939 (renewed 1967) by Condé Nast Publications Inc.

Pages 59, 61. Photographs by the author.

Page 62. Photograph by Ping Amranand.

Page 63. Photograph by Alexander Wallace. Copyright 1991 Alexander L. Wallace. Courtesy of Historic Charleston Foundation.

Page 64. Photograph by the author.

Pages 65, 66, 67, 68, 69. Photographs by Alexander Wallace. Copyright 1991 Alexander L. Wallace.

Pages 71, 72, 73. Photographs by the author.

Pages 74, 75, 76–77. Photographs by Alexander Wallace. Copyright 1991 Alexander L. Wallace.

Pages 78, 79. Photographs and plan by the author.

Pages 80, 81 (top). Photographs by Alexander

Wallace. Copyright 1991 Alexander L. Wallace.

Page 81 (bottom). Photograph by the author.

Page 82. Illustration based on garden plan by Hugh Dargan Associates.

Page 83. Photographs by Alexander Wallace. Copyright 1991 Alexander L. Wallace.

Page 84, 85 (bottom). Photographs by the author.

Pages 85 (top). Photograph by Alexander Wallace. Copyright 1991 Alexander L. Wallace.

Page 86. Illustration based on garden plan by Hugh Dargan Associates.

Page 87. Photograph by Alexander Wallace. Copyright 1991 Alexander L. Wallace.

Pages 88, 89, 90 (top). Photographs by Alexander Wallace. Copyright 1991 Alexander L. Wallace.

Page 90 (bottom). Illustration based on garden plan by Hugh Dargan Associates.

Page 91 (top). Photograph by Alexander Wallace. Copyright 1991 Alexander L. Wallace.

Page 91 (bottom). Photograph by Derek Fell.

Page 92. Copyright 1990 Southern Living, Inc. Reprinted with permission.

Page 93. Photographs by Alexander Wallace. Copyright 1991 Alexander L. Wallace.

Page 94. Copyright 1990 Southern Living, Inc. Reprinted with permission.

Page 95. Photographs by Alexander Wallace. Copyright 1991 Alexander L. Wallace.

Page 96. Illustration based on garden plans by Hugh Dargan Associates and by Emma Richardson for the Charleston Museum.

Page 97. Photographs by the author.

Pages 99, 100, 101. Photographs by the author.

Pages 102–3. Photograph by Alexander Wallace. Copyright 1991 Alexander L. Wallace.

Pages 103 (right top, right bottom), 104, 105, 106. Photographs by the author.

Page 107. Photograph by Alexander Wallace. Copyright 1991 Alexander L. Wallace.

Pages 108, 109, 110, 111. Photographs by the author.

Page 113. Courtesy of Maritime Heritage Prints.

Page 115. Illustration from John James Audubon's *The Birds of America.* Courtesy of the Charleston Museum, Charleston, S.C.

Page 116. Illustration from *Flore médicale* (1814–20) by F. P. Chaumeton. Courtesy of Hunt Institute of Botanical Documentation, Carnegie Mellon University, Pittsburgh, Penn.

All photographs on pages 117–32 and 134–52 are by the author.

Page 133. Photograph by Derek Fell.